EVERYMAN,
I WILL GO WITH THEE,
AND BE THY GUIDE,
IN THY MOST NEED
TO GO BY THY SIDE

EVELYN WAUGH

Decline and Fall

EVERYMAN'S LIBRARY
Alfred A. Knopf New York Toronto

156

THIS IS A BORZOI BOOK

PUBLISHED BY ALFRED A. KNOPF, INC.

Copyright © 1928 by Evelyn Waugh
Copyright renewed © 1956 by Evelyn Waugh
First included in Everyman's Library, 1993
Published by arrangement with Little, Brown and Company
Introduction, Bibliography and Chronology Copyright © 1993 by
David Campbell Publishers Ltd.
Typography by Peter B. Willberg

ISBN 0-679-42041-X
LC 92-54285

Library of Congress Cataloging-in-Publication Data
Waugh, Evelyn, 1903–1966.
Decline and fall / Evelyn Waugh.
p.   cm.—(Everyman's library)
ISBN 0-679-42041-X : $15.00 ($19.00 Can.)
I. Title.
PR6045.A97D4   1993   92-54285
823'.912—dc20   CIP

Printed and bound in Germany

INTRODUCTION

In 1943 the distinguished American critic Edmund Wilson belatedly read *Decline and Fall*. No Anglophile, he had ignored it for fifteen years. Now that he had got round to it he confessed that he was delighted, especially with 'that hair-raising harlequinade in a brazenly bad boys' school' at the beginning of the book. The latter part of the book, he thought, leaned a little too heavily on Voltaire's *Candide*, but his regret at this falling-off did not prevent him from crediting the novel with the virtues of 'spontaneity' and 'audacity'. Not long afterwards *Brideshead Revisited* appeared and Wilson found it a serious disappointment; in his opinion the author had simply lost his way, or perhaps his audacity and spontaneity. There is certainly room for disagreement about the merits of *Brideshead Revisited*, though it should be acknowledged that despite its relative heaviness and a certain sentimentality it is, like all Waugh's books, a novel of undoubted individuality and power. On the other hand most readers would accept without much demur Wilson's judgment of *Decline and Fall* and its pre-war successors, *Vile Bodies*, *Black Mischief*, *A Handful of Dust*, and *Scoop*.

'Spontaneity' and 'audacity', though not inaccurate characterizations, are nevertheless inadequate. One needs at least to add 'hilarity', and even that does not quite cover the case. Waugh himself once made the point that hilarity is by no means necessarily an accompaniment or product of happiness. The audacities of his first novel – written when he was twenty-five – are touched by the first hints of a farcical desperation that will increase with time. His hilarity – or rather, his power to produce hilarity in the reader, for *Decline and Fall* is a book that for over fifty years has retained its ability to make readers writhe with laughter – has a certain dark, even menacing quality. For example, nobody could possibly mistake *Decline and Fall* for one of Wodehouse's deftly, daftly plotted tales. That world of genial innocence, in which crafty servants, descended from ancestors in Roman comedy, do the necessary thinking for their masters and get them out of scrapes caused by their own incapacities, or by the moral demands of ferocious aunts, is not, except in that both deal with the bizarre adventures of upper-class youth, Waugh's world. One cannot imagine Bertie Wooster reduced to prep-school teaching or expect to find in Wodehouse an aristocratic entrepreneur who owns a chain of Latin American brothels; and nobody in Waugh lives in a near-paradise like Blandings. There is no such earthly paradise in Waugh, and anything approaching that dignity is either an illusion or a thing of the past. Any houses that could be thought by their old-fashioned owners to have a claim to that title are pulled down, as Margot Beste-Chetwynde destroys King's Thursday, or as Brenda Last, in *A Handful of Dust*, sets in train the ruin of Hetton. Such acts of vandalism, along with many other dreadful but amusing instances of modern irresponsibility, provide reasons or excuses for the melancholy that gives Waugh's hilarity its peculiar resonance.

Evelyn Waugh later constructed an elaborate myth of lost Catholic aristocracy, founded on the fact, indubitable though of varying significance depending on where, as to religion, you stand, that English patrician families had at some point in the past, and notably under Henry VIII, fallen into apostasy. He himself was born into a secure Protestant middle-class professional family. His father was a respected publisher, his elder brother a successful writer. He suffered the education proper to his class, in preparatory and public schools of impeccable though not magnificent status. He was to remark that such an education at least enabled people to accept prison conditions more cheerfully than the lower classes.

Oxford in the post-war years, the epoch celebrated in the first pages of *Brideshead Revisited*, was for him, as for many, a wonderful relief, and he found there congenially dissipated companions, some of them much richer and grander than he. There were among them those who, tolerating his gloomier eccentricities, remained his friends in later years.

Following an academically inglorious Oxford career he took for a time the course, not unusual for lively but impecunious academic failures, of becoming a preparatory school teacher.

INTRODUCTION

Though it brought him rewards he could not have foreseen at the time, this was hardly the career he would have chosen. He found piecework in London, writing for the journals, working briefly for the paper he later exploited under the name of the *Daily Excess*. Meanwhile he kept up a serious interest in art, being himself a talented draughtsman. He attended an art school, though briefly, and at one time he thought of apprenticing himself to a cabinet maker. Thus did the influence of William Morris survive into the era of Ronald Firbank.

He was attracted by the Pre-Raphaelite Brotherhood, and his first extended piece of writing was an essay on that group, privately printed in 1926. Pursuing that interest, he published in 1928 his first book, a biography of Gabriel Rossetti – a competent work which was received with respect. Its sobriety is in strong contrast to the mood of *Decline and Fall*, which was published later in the same year. Christopher Sykes, in his biography of Waugh, makes the ingenious suggestion that Rossetti and his circle appealed to Waugh not only because he liked their work but because he saw in Rossetti's insomnia and drugtaking an image or prediction of his own fate. At any rate the existence of this sober twin of *Decline and Fall* reminds us that Waugh could be simultaneously serious and hilarious – not that *Rossetti* is at all dull. Waugh was right to note in his diary that it was 'quite amusing in parts'.

Another diary note, dated 3 September 1927, records that he had 'begun on a comic novel'. Despite his apparently rather hectic social life he must have applied himself to its writing the same speed and efficiency that, as the diaries suggest, he showed when working on *Rossetti*. By the time of his first marriage, in June of the following year, he was reading proof. Early in October 1928 he noted that he had seen *Decline and Fall* on a best-seller list; but although there was a second printing in that month print runs were small, and the sales were in fact rather modest. For a more satisfying success, attended by a measure of notoriety, he had to wait until the publication, early in 1930, of *Vile Bodies*. By then he had suffered a peculiarly bitter experience in his own life, for his marriage had abruptly ended. *Vile Bodies* is a wilder book than *Decline and Fall*, a comic vision of the sort of people who by their mode of life bring upon themselves enormous calamities. The tone of dark hilarity continues in *Black Mischief* (1932), and persists two years later in Waugh's sombre yet still funny masterpiece, *A Handful of Dust*.

*

Decline and Fall fantasticates many personal experiences and has many in-jokes, some of them presumably inaccessible to anybody outside a very small circle of friends. However, they do no harm. Waugh had a mischievous habit of introducing the names of people he had met, and distributing them with apparent irrelevance among his characters. Philbrick, conferred on that fantastically versatile criminal, the butler at Llanaba, was the name of an Oxford undergraduate contemporary with Waugh, who, as it appears, had for some reason given him the nickname of 'Philbrick the Flagellant'; it caught on, and under severe provocation the injured Philbrick revenged himself by assaulting its author. The name Fagan, awarded to the Headmaster of Llanaba, had belonged to a young woman whom Waugh had introduced, disguised as a boy, into a strictly male Oxford party. The burglar Crutwell is named after the Dean of Waugh's college; he disliked Waugh, who detested him in return, and ensured that his name would be attached to some unlikeable character in every novel up to *Scoop*. Crutwell is still remembered, the loathing only slightly mitigated by compassion – he is described as 'a wreck of the war' – in Waugh's autobiography, *A Little Learning*. More obviously, Jack Spire of *The London Hercules* is Sir John Squire of *The London Mercury*, whom Waugh had met.

The first edition of the novel was illustrated by some of Waugh's own drawings, and one of them depicts the brothel quarter of Marseilles, which he had visited with his brother Alec. In this drawing one *louche* establishment bears the sign 'Chez Otoline' – a jest which Lady Ottoline Morrell, a famous literary hostess, either missed or thought fit to ignore. Some names, Miles Malpractice for instance, are substitutes for others which, being too pointed, too identifiable, were changed at the request of the publisher. Other persons, some well known, appear under names which do not resemble their real ones, for example David Lennox, the fashionable photographer, is recognizable as Cecil Beaton. The games with nomenclature, along with the deft verbal caricatures, reflect that passion for teases and practical jokes which also animated and gave the characteristic quality of outrage to Waugh's comic plots.

There are more innocent borrowings. The grammatical definition Paul Pennyfeather finds in the textbook given him to read in prison – 'a syllable is a single sound made by one effort of the voice' – is an example drawn from work Waugh himself set for a class of dull students at Arnold House, the preparatory school in Wales where he taught for two terms in 1925. That dreary experience was, as it turned out, an essential preparation for the writing of *Decline and Fall*. For Arnold House, one need hardly add, is the original of Llanaba Castle.

In his autobiography and in his diaries Waugh has quite a lot to say about his time there, and some of his remarks may surprise readers of *Decline and Fall*. In his pre-fictional accounts of the school he calls it 'depressingly well conducted'. It is true that he failed to win the respect of the headmaster's powerful wife, 'Mrs Vanhomrigh' – pronounced, he explains, 'Vanummery'. In fact her name was Banks; why, in a supposedly factual account, he gave her the unusual name of Swift's friend Hester Vanhomrigh I have not seen explained. There is evidence that Mr Banks was no Fagan but a perfectly sane and respectable schoolmaster, and that Waugh himself, though perhaps not a very effective teacher, was at least popular with the boys. So much can be gathered from the testimony of the writer Derek Verschoyle, who was a pupil at Arnold House when Waugh was there. He provided Christopher Sykes with a rather elegant account of his schooldays, and of his relations with Waugh, whom he found quite amiable, though useless at games. One of the new master's prescribed tasks was to teach Verschoyle to play the organ, an instrument with which Waugh was unfamiliar. Readers of *Decline and Fall* will remember that Paul Pennyfeather is likewise required to teach young Beste-Chetwynde the organ, and that their relationship, though friendly, had grave consequences for Penny-feather. It led to his involvement with Beste-Chetwynde's mother Margot, later Lady Metroland, who planned but failed to marry him, and instead allowed him to be arrested and imprisoned for offences very much hers and not his. Thus, it seems, did plausible fragments of memory cohere to form fantastic jokes and plots.

Waugh says that when he was starting the novel he reread the diaries he kept as a schoolboy at Lancing, and no doubt they were helpful, but his more recent experiences at Arnold House were clearly more important. He fantasticated them, writing rapidly but with the fastidious care that is character-istic of all his work. It is visible in the plotting, in the dialogue, and in the writing of every sentence. His highest claim, put forward with a kind of proud modesty, was to good craftman-ship; his stated aim in writing novels was to make finely finished objects, like a good cabinet maker. The remarkable quasi-autobiographical passage at the beginning of his novella *The Ordeal of Gilbert Pinfold* (1957) is perfectly just: 'It may happen in the next hundred years that the English novelist of the present day will come to be valued as we now value the artists and craftsmen of the late eighteenth century ... Among these novelists Mr Gilbert Pinfold stood quite high.' Mr Pinfold claims for his books is that they are 'well made'. But he admits that craft alone may not be enough, that the novelist needs also a touch of the demonic. Pinfold–Waugh had this gift also. Pinfold in his sickness weaves paranoid fantasies that strike the reader, though not, on the whole, Pinfold, as hilarious. Waugh deployed in fiction all the comical social prejudices, as well as the taste for ruthless teasing and practical joking, with which, in life, he assaulted others as well as himself. But however demonic or fantastic the motive, the product must be well made. One feature of the craftsmanlike, the well-made, is that it is manifestly so, there is no need to boast about it; and, that one still modest passage in *Pinfold* apart, Waugh hardly ever does so. Equally there should be no appearance of labour; yet we know that he did revise and polish, not least when writing *Decline and Fall*.

One instance of such revision is the character of Mr Grimes.

Alternately in the soup and landing on his feet, he weaves his way through the book, rather as the absconding bounderish major will do in *Vile Bodies* – sometimes gloomy, always threatened, but in the end a rather heroic survivor. He is the sort perhaps more often met in the interwar years than before or after, hanging on and making a living somehow – marginal, unscrupulous, likeable, almost 'a capital fellow' ('capital fellows *are* bounders' as Waugh, who knew many of them and celebrated some, himself remarked). Grimes is based on a master at Arnold House, whose bounderishness at first amused Waugh, though he soon decided he was boring. The distance between this person and Grimes was indeed considerable; as the story developed the fictional character acquired a glory and a pathos that removed him far from his original. In the earliest version of the novel Grimes, like his model, was candidly a pederast, having a special relationship with young Clutterbuck. Only discreet traces of his pederasty remain in the final version, as when Grimes fixes the heats on the day before the school sports, giving Clutterbuck many victories ('he's a splendid little athlete'). They may be more effective for being unobtrusive, and indeed would hardly, in 1928, have been condoned if they had been otherwise.

Waugh's first idea was to have Grimes flee from the understandably repellent prospect of marriage to Fagan's daughter, only to be decapitated by the Irish Mail as it roared through Llanaba station. But he came to see that what he needed was not a defunct Grimes, who carelessly lost his head just as, earlier, he had lost his leg, but a Grimes who always emerged from the soup and landed on his feet, who had the marvellous durability of the genuine bounder. In his usual ruthless way he transferred the fate of decapitation to silly, unbounderish Prendergast, who became the victim of the foolishly liberal policies, deplored by Pennyfeather and also, we feel, by the author, of a wet prison governor. And so Grimes escapes and inevitably turns up at King's Thursday to join the white slave racket.

Turning up is of course, a structural device in *Decline and Fall*: Philbrick is everywhere, Fagan turns up as boss of the hospital where Paul has his fake operation. Another whose turnings up are introduced with cruel insouciance, is the young Lord Tangent, grazed by a bullet from the pistol lent by Philbrick to Prendergast for use as a starting pistol at the phoney sports. Later we are casually informed that the foot has swollen up and turned black; then that it has been amputated. Some time after that we learn of the boy's death (which, as it happens, he himself predicted at the outset: 'Am I going to die?') and of the lamentations of his mother, Lady Circumference, described in *Vile Bodies* as 'the organ voice of England, the hunting-cry of the *ancien régime*'. 'It's maddenin' Tangent having died just at this time,' she says, fearing that people may wrongly suppose the death of her son to be the reason for her declining to attend Margot Beste-Chetwynde's second wedding.

So it goes: chance collisons, absurd but some times fatal sequences of incident, in a small world where it is useless to seek a rational or just concatenation of events, or an account of human relations dictated by probability or decency. In *Vile Bodies* the cosmopolitan Jesuit Fr Rothschild is permitted to observe that the behaviour of modern youth arises from 'a fatal hunger for permanence', a piece of moralizing Waugh seems later to have regretted. Certainly there is nothing of the kind in *Decline and Fall*. There the young vandalize, fornicate, cheat at cards. In a Victorian novel such as Trollope's *The Way We Live Now* we would be invited to experience distaste or horror at such goings-on; fornication is beyond forgiveness, almost beyond mention, and even cheating at cards is treated with unqualified dismay. There is in Trollope's novel a young man, Sir Felix Carbury, member of a very smart, very corrupt set, who by sleeping in after a debauch omits to elope with an heiress. One can just about imagine what Waugh would have made of that situation, and indeed of the young man; in Trollope he is made out to be uniformly detestable, but Waugh, even if his treatment allowed us to think likewise of Sir Felix, would not himself have said so.

It is not only the very young who escape; their elders – white slave traders, vain and useless politicians, adulterers, epicene photographers, inhuman architects – are not censured. Indeed all these people are made more interesting than Paul Pennyfeather. Only the dull are honest, perhaps for want of wit. Paul, though impelled by chance events into association with so fast a set, is not qualified to belong to it, as Peter Pastmaster lets him know at the end. He travels impassively through a world of deception, folly, treachery and fraud, a world in which the rituals of punishment are as meaningless as those of love. If the proper responses to such a world are either despair or hilarity he displays neither. He is simply manipulated by it, and he does not belong. Yet he doesn't belong, either, with Prendergast, who is much more naive and stupid.

Paul's world is, or ought to be, that of his friend Potts, with whom he exchanges serious letters. Yet Potts's association with the boringly worthy League of Nations causes him to betray his friend. There is a sense in which the characters of *Decline and Fall* are divided into those who are strong, careless sinners, those who do not count at all, and those who, like Paul, are neither hot nor cold, who are not strong or assured enough to sin but whose innocence is not of a kind to ensure that they acquire merit.

Paul is certainly a kind of Candide, a victim, unresisting, unvirtuous. He has no Pangloss, no absurd philosopher, to advise him, though he does seem to accept that, such as it is, venal and absurd as it is, the world in which he finds himself is the best of all possible worlds. In the opening scene, the Bollinger gang, not exactly reading men, roar, break windows, smash china, deface a Matisse, destroy a piano, stone a fox to death with champagne bottles, and so on. Yet when they attack Paul it is he, not they, who suffers at the hands of the authorities; their removal of his trousers exposed him to a capital charge of indecency. Sent down by the comically venal dons, he accepts his fate without effective protest – he is even ashamed of himself for saying 'God damn and blast them to hell' as he ignominiously departs – just as he accepts with resignation the disastrous consequences of the glass-breaker Alastair Digby-Vaine-Trumpington's later interventions in his life. When Dr Fagan asks him why he left the university so suddenly he accurately, but without using available excuses, admits that he was sent down for indecent behaviour; Fagan finds the confession a reason for reducing Paul's exiguous salary. He replies in exactly the same way when questioned by Prendergast.

In love with Margot, he is ignorant and incurious about her trade, easily becomes a scapegoat, and is condemned as very wicked, a distinction he doesn't deserve. He hardly seems to resent his luck, and enjoys the rigours of prison, especially solitary confinement. When the treacherous Margot finally visited him to explain that their marriage is off, he was 'greatly pained to find how little he was pained' by the news. No doubt there is here some reflection of the feeling, not uncommon at a time when the Great War was a recent memory, that one was simply at the mercy of forces uncontrollable by the individual will; yet to feel that is to be the type of personality known as Laodicean: lukewarm, neither cold nor hot. We are allowed to think Paul's destiny appropriate; reinstated as a humble student of divinity, he enjoys reading about outrageous and fiercely condemned ancient heresies. 'Quite right to suppress them.' Here at last was a world which made some sense without threatening or involving him personally in its wickedness and its retributions.

Such interests are not so remote from Waugh's own as might be thought. Paul, reading about ancient heresies in Scone, is imitating or parodying John Henry Newman, who spent a long vacation in Oxford reading about the Monophysites, and so for the first time came to doubt 'the tenableness of Anglicanism': 'here,' he wrote in *Apologia Pro Vita Sua*, 'in the middle of the fifth century I found, as it seemed to me, Christendom of the sixteenth and nineteenth century, reflected. I saw my face in that mirror and I was a Monophysite.' Heresy and apostasy were prominent among Waugh's later overt preoccupations, though he was never, as Newman may have been for a moment, a Monophysite (believing that Christ had only one nature).

After his conversion to Rome he was able to give expression to his quite orthodox religious preoccupations, for example in *Helena* (1950), a novel about St Helena, daughter of the British King Cole, mother of the first Christian emperor Constantine, and discoverer of the True Cross. The pure factuality of Catholic Christianity, symbolized by the plain unadorned wood of the Cross, was the true reality; anything else masquerading as that was absurd or a fraud. Departures from the Christian facts – by other religions, from the hot-gospelling of *Vile Bodies* and the foot-reading of *A Handful of Dust* to what was called, with much distaste, 'humanism' – were heresies, and those who professed them were apostates; it would be quite right to suppress them if, in this less satisfactory age, that were possible. In later life he came to believe that even the Vatican was betraying the truth; the abandonment of the Latin mass distressed him greatly.

But an enjoyment of human absurdity, including his own, long sustained him. It is brilliantly evident in *Pinfold*. He still loathed apostasy, including its secular variants, and he could hardly approve of the bounders who apostasized from honour in the evacuation of Crete. His war trilogy indeed contains many bounders; few of them are capital fellows but they are still very amusing.

His final diary entries have still a sardonic wit, occasionally associated with a bold declaration of Catholic truth in circumstances where others might not think to find it in evidence. Writing of Timothy Evans, a man of subnormal intelligence executed for a murder he did not commit, he comments that Evans, a lapsed Catholic, had been hell-bent until his conviction, when he returned to the faith and 'died shriven'. Himself bored almost to death, he was still witty: 'All fates are worse than death,' he noted. There is something about such observations, though they doubtless reflect a deeply held conviction, that reminds one of absurd and unfair destinies described in the novels – the fate, for instance, of little Lord Tangent, or of Prudence in *Black Mischief*, who is inadvertently eaten at a cannibal feast by her lover Basil Seal. Presumably she was unshriven at the time.

In Muriel Spark's story 'The Portobello Road' a girl is murdered; and another woman reacts to the news by exclaiming how lucky the victim was to have been to confession the night before. She is said to be 'speaking from that Catholic point of view which takes some getting used to'. This is true enough, and in some ways novels written from that point of view also take some getting used to. Waugh himself presumably would have had no difficulty with the idea that the murdered girl had been lucky, and would also have agreed with Mrs Spark, whom he warmly admired, that there is some active but obscure relation between fictive plots and a divine plot that is absolutely true but which we cannot understand.

Why, it may be asked, does God allow dirty tricks in his scenario for the world, as when Jacob–Israel cheats Esau out of his blessing? Why is Hosea commanded to marry a prostitute? Why does Samson have to marry two unsatisfactory gentiles and have his eyes put out to ensure the defeat of the Philistines? Why are the four women named in Matthew's genealogy of Jesus all in one way or another apparently unsuitable? And so on. Mrs Spark reflects on such matters when considering the divine purpose of a bitterly divided Jerusalem in *The Mandelbaum Gate*. As to Jacob's treachery, she remarks that 'the mighty blessing, once bestowed, was irrevocable', and that God has no interest in fair play; he wasn't, as she comments, educated at Eton. Another Catholic novelist, Graham Greene, at any rate in some moods, like that prevailing in *The End of the Affair*, also, though more gloomily, contemplates the apparently irrational and sometimes cruel incursions of grace into the lives of sinners, arbitrarily determining their plots and their fates.

Decline and Fall was of course written before Waugh's conversion, but with hindsight we can think of it as Catholic *avant la lettre*; it plays many tricks of the sort Mrs Spark is thinking about. Moments of decision or indecision, of no significance on a human scale of values, turn out to have immense importance. Paul, on his wedding day drinks a toast to Fortune and then stays on, slightly against his better judgment, for another drink with his evil angel Alastair; so he is still there, as he need not have been, when the police arrive to arrest him. Even then he does not understand the extent of the catastrophe this trivial slip entails; it is left to the boy Peter Pastmaster to do that. Or think of Prendergast, victim of the good intentions of the liberalizing prison governor; how appropriate that news of his death should be passed around to the tune of 'O God our help in ages past'.

If you accept that the world is a fallen world, subject to apparently random and wanton intrusions of sense or reality, it becomes easier to accept as hilarious what otherwise seems rather to be a cause for despair. At the time of *Decline and Fall* Waugh would probably not have expressed a view of fiction similar to Muriel Spark's, but it happened that his kind of writing, and the assumptions on which it was based, were consonant with a view of that sort, and the deeper structure of his plots was to become more evident in later work. Thus, as I say by hindsight, we can make this first novel out to be Catholic. Of course he might have explained Esau's disappointment differently, perhaps as what was deserved for being thick, or a bore, like Sir Humphrey Maltravers, or a wimp like Prendergast, or a crook like the bishop, Prendy's patron, who approved of 'modern churchmen who drew their pay without the necessity of commitment to any religious belief'.

Waugh's novel has in common with the relevant chapters of Genesis that, as Grimes remarks when he arrives at King's Thursday to get in on the 'places of entertainment' racket, it is a small world. With the larger world, with society more largely considered – the idea of a larger community, requiring concern for unemployment, homelessness, famine – Waugh had very little to do; like Mrs Thatcher, he hardly believed there was such a thing as society in that sense. So Virginia Woolf's remark that Waugh's early satire showed no interest in social conditions was true enough. It was important to him, however, to have a view of the social order which provided him with social (and no doubt racial) inferiors. The poor he expected, he said, to cheat and lie, though presumably they did so less interestingly than the rich. His plots avoided all considerations of general welfare; they reflected Jacob's inspired fraud, making no provision for the indigence of stupid Esau. You can't help feeling that in *Decline and Fall* the narrator is not on the side of Pennyfeather, nor on that of the greedy dons, nor on that of the forces of law and order. His affection for the likes of Alastair Digby-Vaine-Trumpington is evident from that character's reappearances. (In *Put Out More Flags* he joins up as a private, ostensibly to avoid contact with middle-class temporary officers, though – it is suggested – really as a penance. Presumably there is no such penitential benefit for proletarian conscripts.)

Conscience of the ordinary kind is represented, in the earlier books, as an unenviable possession of the middle classes. Paul is the sort of person who might occasionally feel a twinge of it. Trumpington had, with aristocratic insouciance, deprived him of his entire income, and, measuring Paul's worth, had offered him compensation of twenty pounds. Thereupon Paul has a crisis in which he undergoes what he supposes to be the struggle of conscience appropriate to his social position. He believes that 'by any ordinary process of thought, the money is justly mine. But ... there is my honour. For generations the British bourgeoisie have spoken of themselves as gentlemen, and by that they have meant, among other things, a self-respecting scorn of irregular perquisites. It is the quality that distinguishes the gentleman from both the artist and the aristocrat. ... Now I am a gentleman. I can't help it: it's born in me. I just can't take the money.' Paul, thus tamely distancing himself from his aristocratic friends (and from the artist who is writing the passage?) is quickly corrected by Grimes, who, despite his dubious origins, has the proper instincts of aristocrat or artist. He has already got the twenty pounds; Paul gets his small blessing whether he wants it or not. Grimes of course is a gentleman too, a public school man, but has learned how to live with it.

I have never been quite happy about his performance – his 'agony' – at the dinner given by Paul in the Hotel Metropole at Cwmprydygg. It is understandable that he should take a poor view of marriage, but this philosophizing sounds out of character: 'There's a home and family waiting for every one of us. We can't escape, try as we may. It's the seed of life we carry about with us like our skeletons, each of us unconsciously pregnant with desirable villa residences ...' Grimes is surely pregnant rather with 'places of entertainment', and so finds himself more at home in the ambience of the Beste-Chetwyndes than Paul does; and unlike Paul, when he wants out he can always arrange it.

Philbrick is another independent figure, crossing all boundaries: butler, millionaire, intimate of the famous criminal Crutwell; a creature adapted to this world. So is Dr Fagan, professional snob, benign monster of prejudice: 'from the earliest times the Welsh have been looked on as an unclean people. It is thus that they have preserved their racial integrity. Their sons and daughters rarely mate with humankind except their own blood relations.' This is outrageous, but so is the whole book. Like Dr Fagan we 'look forward to each new fiasco with the utmost relish'. In a world providing a preview of chaos theory there are fiascos in plenty, arising, often enough, from apparently trivial causes, and related to one another by a sort of demonic craftsmanship.

Decline and Fall is full of distinctive voices and distinctively absurd ways of behaving, all beautifully interrelated. Hindsight may enable us to find in it the promise of narratives both more hilarious and more solemn to come, but it is itself an original masterpiece. It is clear evidence for the truth of the praise its author awarded himself in the opening pages of *Pinfold*: he undoubtedly stood 'quite high' among the most gifted craftsmen of his time.

Frank Kermode

SELECT BIBLIOGRAPHY

THE NOVELS OF EVELYN WAUGH
(all published by Chapman & Hall and by Little, Brown)

Decline and Fall, 1928.
Vile Bodies, 1930.
Black Mischief, 1932.
A Handful of Dust, 1934.
Scoop, 1938.
Put Out More Flags, 1942.
Brideshead Revisited, 1945.
The Loved One, 1948.
Helena, 1950.
Men at Arms, 1952.
Officers and Gentlemen, 1955.
The Ordeal of Gilbert Pinfold, 1957.
Unconditional Surrender, 1961.
(*Men at Arms*, *Officers and Gentlemen*, and *Unconditional Surrender* form a
trilogy later published in a revised version as *Sword of Honour*, 1965.)

STORIES

Mr Loveday's Little Outing and other sad stories, 1936.
Work Suspended and other stories, 1949.
(Both published by Chapman & Hall)
Charles Ryder's Schooldays and other stories, Little, Brown.

BIOGRAPHY

Rossetti, his Life and Works, Duckworth, 1928.
Edmund Campion: Jesuit and Martyr, Longman, 1935.
The Life of the Right Reverend Ronald Knox, Chapman & Hall, 1959.

TRAVEL

Labels. A Mediterranean Journey, Duckworth, 1930.
Remote People, Duckworth, 1931, and Ecco Press.
Ninety-two Days, Duckworth, 1934.
Waugh in Abyssinia, Longman, Green & Co., 1936.
Robbery Under Law: The Mexican Object-Lesson, Chapman & Hall, 1939.
When the Going Was Good, Duckworth, 1946, and Little, Brown.
A Tourist in Africa, Chapman & Hall, 1960.

AUTOBIOGRAPHY

A Little Learning. The First Volume of an Autobiography, Chapman & Hall, 1964, and Little, Brown.

LETTERS

The Letters of Evelyn Waugh, ed. Mark Amory, Weidenfeld and Nicolson, 1980.

DIARIES

The Diaries of Evelyn Waugh, ed. Michael Davie, Weidenfeld and Nicolson, 1976.

ESSAYS etc.

The Essays, Articles and Reviews of Evelyn Waugh, ed. Donat Gallagher, Methuen, 1983, and Little, Brown.

BIOGRAPHIES

STANNARD, MARTIN, *Evelyn Waugh. The Early Years, 1903-1939*, Dent, 1986, and W. W. Norton.
—*Evelyn Waugh: No Abiding City, 1939-1966*, Dent, 1992, and W. W. Norton.
SYKES, CHRISTOPHER, *Evelyn Waugh: A Biography*, Collins, 1975.

CRITICISM

STANNARD, MARTIN, *Evelyn Waugh: The Critical Heritage*, Routledge & Kegan Paul, London and New York, 1984.

C H R O N O L O G Y

DATE	AUTHOR'S LIFE	LITERARY CONTEXT
1897	Birth of Alec Waugh, Evelyn's brother.	
1903	Birth of Evelyn Waugh to Arthur and Catherine Waugh in Hampstead.	James: *The Ambassadors.* Shaw: *Man and Superman.*
1904		James: *The Golden Bowl.* Conrad: *Nostromo.*
1907		Conrad: *The Secret Agent.*
1908		Forster: *A Room with a View.* Bennett: *The Old Wives' Tale.*
1910	Attends Heath Mount preparatory school. *The Curse of the Horse Race* (unpublished).	Forster: *Howards End.*
1911		Lawrence: *The White Peacock.*
1913		Lawrence: *Sons and Lovers.* Proust: *A la Recherche du Temps Perdu.*
1914		Conrad: *Chance.* Joyce: *Dubliners.*
1915		Madox Ford: *The Good Soldier.* Conrad: *Victory.* Buchan: *The Thirty-Nine Steps.* Woolf: *The Voyage Out.*
1916	Attends Lancing College. Starts to write diaries which continue throughout his life.	Joyce: *A Portrait of the Artist as a Young Man.* Shaw: *Pygmalion.*
1917		Yeats: *The Wild Swans at Coole.* Eliot: *Prufrock and Other Observations.*
1918		Brooke: *Collected Poems.* Pirandello: *Six Characters in Search of an Author.*
1919		Shaw: *Heartbreak House.*
1920		Pound: *Hugh Selwyn Mauberley.*
1921	Attends Hertford College, Oxford; also studies at the Ruskin School of Art.	Huxley: *Crome Yellow.*

HISTORICAL EVENTS

Emmeline Pankhurst founds the Women's Social and Political Union.

Russo-Japanese war.

Asquith becomes Prime Minister.
Death of Edward VII. Liberals back in power.

Coronation of George V. Agadir crisis. Suffragette riots.

Outbreak of World War I.
Asquith forms coalition government with Balfour.

First battle of the Somme. Lloyd George becomes Prime Minister.

Russian revolution. US joins war. Third battle of Ypres.

Armistice. Women over thirty gain vote.

Versailles peace conference.
League of Nations formed. Prohibition in the US.

DATE	AUTHOR'S LIFE	LITERARY CONTEXT
1922		Joyce: *Ulysses*.
		Eliot: *The Waste Land*.
		Housman: *Last Poems*.
		Fitzgerald: *The Beautiful and the Damned*.
1923	*Anthony, Who Sought Things That Were Lost*.	e e cummings: *The Enormous Room*.
		Huxley: *Antic Hay*.
1924	Leaves Oxford with a third class honours degree. Waugh then becomes a master at a preparatory school. *The Temple at Thatch* (unpublished).	Forster: *A Passage to India*.
		Shaw: *Saint Joan*.
1925		Fitzgerald: *The Great Gatsby*.
		Kafka: *The Trial*.
1926	Trains as a carpenter. *P.R.B. An Essay on the Pre-Raphaelite Brotherhood* (printed privately). *The Balance* (Georgian Papers).	Faulkner: *Soldiers' Pay*.
		Nabokov: *Mary*.
		Henry Green: *Blindness*.
1927	Meets and marries Evelyn Gardner. Publishes his first book, a biography of Dante Gabriel Rossetti.	Woolf: *To the Lighthouse*.
		Hemingway: *Men Without Women*.
		Dunne: *An Experiment with Time*.
1928	*Decline and Fall*.	Lawrence: *Lady Chatterley's Lover*.
		Woolf: *Orlando*.
		Yeats: *The Tower*.
		Lewis: *The Childermass*.
		Nabokov: *King, Queen, Knave*.
1929	Divorces his wife Evelyn.	Faulkner: *The Sound and the Fury*.
		Cocteau: *Les Enfants Terribles*.
		Hemingway: *A Farewell to Arms*.
		Priestley: *The Good Companions*.
		Remarque: *All Quiet on the Western Front*.
1930	Converts to Roman Catholicism. *Vile Bodies, Labels*.	Eliot: *Ash Wednesday*.
		Faulkner: *As I Lay Dying*.
		Nabokov: *The Defence*.
1931	Travels around Africa and South America. *Remote People*.	Faulkner: *Sanctuary*.

CHRONOLOGY

HISTORICAL EVENTS

Stalin becomes General Secretary of the Communist party Central Committee. Mussolini marches on Rome. Coalition falls and Bonar Law forms Conservative ministry.

Baldwin becomes Prime Minister. Hitler's coup in Munich fails. Women gain legal equality in divorce suits.

First Labour government formed by Ramsay McDonald. Hitler in prison. Death of Lenin. Baldwin becomes Prime Minister again after a Conservative election victory.

Locarno conference.

British general strike. First television demonstrated. Stalin begins to oust Trotsky. French financial crisis.

German economy collapses.

Hoover becomes US president.

Wall Street crash.

Gandhi begins civil disobedience campaign in India. Nazis win seats from the moderates in German election.

DATE	AUTHOR'S LIFE	LITERARY CONTEXT
1932	*Black Mischief, Cruise, Bella Fleace Gave a Party, Incident in Azania.*	Huxley: *Brave New World.* Faulkner: *Light in August.* Nabokov: *Glory.*
1933	*Out of Depth.*	Malraux: *La Condition Humaine.* Stein: *The Autobiography of Alice B. Toklas.*
1934	*A Handful of Dust, Mr. Loveday's Little Outing, On Guard, Ninety-Two Days.*	
1935	*Winner Takes All,* also a biography of Edmund Campion.	Isherwood: *Mr. Norris Changes Trains.* Eliot: *Murder in the Cathedral.* Odets: *Waiting for Lefty.* Graham Greene: *England Made Me.*
1936	*Period Piece, Excursion in Reality, Waugh in Abyssinia, Love in the Slumps.*	Faulkner: *Absalom, Absalom!* Nabokov: *Despair.*
1937	Marries Laura Herbert.	Hemingway: *To Have and Have Not.* Orwell: *The Road to Wigan Pier.* Sartre: *La Nausée.* Steinbeck: *Of Mice and Men.*
1938	Birth of his daughter Teresa. *Scoop.*	Graham Greene: *Brighton Rock.* Beckett: *Murphy.* Orwell: *Homage to Catalonia.*
1939	Birth of his son Auberon. Joins the Royal Marines and then the Commandos, serving throughout the war. *An Englishman's Home, Robbery Under Law.*	Joyce: *Finnegans Wake.* Eliot: *The Family Reunion.* Steinbeck: *The Grapes of Wrath.* Henry Green: *Party Going.* Auden: *Journey to a War.* Isherwood: *Goodbye to Berlin.*
1940		Hemingway: *For Whom the Bell Tolls.* Graham Greene: *The Power and the Glory.* Dylan Thomas: *Portrait of the Artist as a Young Dog.* Faulkner: *The Hamlet.* Henry Green: *Pack my Bag: A Self-Portrait.*
1941		Acton: *Peonies and Ponies.* Fitzgerald: *The Last Tycoon.*

CHRONOLOGY

HISTORICAL EVENTS

Hunger marches in Britain. F. D. Roosevelt's landslide victory.

Hitler becomes Chancellor of Germany. Nazi persecution of Jews begins.

Riots in Paris.

Italy invades Abyssinia.

Spanish civil war begins. Abdication crisis in Britain.

Japanese invade China. Attempts are made to appease Hitler. Discovery of Fascist plot in Paris. Baldwin retires and Neville Chamberlain becomes Prime Minister.

Germany annexes Austria. Munich crisis.

Germany invades Czechoslovakia and Poland; Britain and France declare war (September 3).

Churchill becomes Prime Minister. France falls and Italy joins the war in alliance with Germany.

USSR is invaded. Japanese attack Pearl Harbor. US joins war.

DATE	AUTHOR'S LIFE	LITERARY CONTEXT
1942	Birth of his daughter Margaret (died 1986). *Put Out More Flags* (a sequel to *Black Mischief*), *Work Suspended*.	Anouilh: *Eurydice*. Sartre: *Les Mouches*. Camus: *L'Etranger*. Camus: *Le Mythe de Sisyphe*.
1943		Davies: *Collected Poems*. Henry Green: *Caught*.
1944	Birth of his daughter Harriet.	Eliot: *Four Quartets*. Anouilh: *Antigone*. Camus: *Caligula*. Sartre: *Huis Clos*.
1945	*Brideshead Revisited, Charles Ryder's School Days*.	Broch: *The Death of Virgil*. Betjeman: *New Bats in Old Belfries*. Orwell: *Animal Farm*. Henry Green: *Loving*.
1946	Birth of his son James. *Scott-King's Modern Europe, When the Going Was Good*.	Rattigan: *The Winslow Boy*. Cocteau: *L'Aigle à Deux Têtes*. Henry Green: *Back*. Dylan Thomas: *Deaths and Entrances*.
1947	*Wine in Peace and War*.	Mann: *Doctor Faustus*. Camus: *La Peste*. Diary of Anne Frank is published. Henry Green: *Concluding*.
1948	*The Loved One*.	Eliot: *Notes Towards the Definition of Culture*. Graham Greene: *The Heart of the Matter*. Faulkner: *Intruder in the Dust*. Henry Green: *Nothing*. Acton: *Memoirs of an Aesthete*.
1949		Orwell: *Nineteen Eighty-Four*. De Beauvoir: *The Second Sex*. Graham Greene: *The Third Man*. Miller: *Death of a Salesman*.
1950	Birth of his son Septimus. *Helena*.	Lawrence Durrell: *Sappho*. Hemingway: *Across the River and into the Trees*. Eliot: *The Cocktail Party*. Henry Green: *Doting*.
1951		Salinger: *The Catcher in the Rye*. Powell: *A Question of Upbringing* (the first of the 12 novels comprising *A Dance to the Music of Time* (1952–75).

CHRONOLOGY

HISTORICAL EVENTS

Germans retreat in Russia, Africa and Italy.

Germany is besieged.

Hitler commits suicide. World War II ends after atom bombs are dropped on Hiroshima and Nagasaki.

Iron curtain speech by Churchill.

Gruppe 47 founded by Young German Writers. Dead Sea scrolls are discovered.

Erhard launches the Deutschemark.

Germany is divided: Adenauer is Chancellor of West Germany, Ulbricht rules East.

Korea declares itself an independent state. Macarthy witch hunts – persecution of Communists throughout US.

DATE	AUTHOR'S LIFE	LITERARY CONTEXT
1952	*Men at Arms*, the first part of the *Sword of Honour* trilogy. *The Holy Places.*	Beckett: *Waiting for Godot.* Miller: *The Crucible.*
1953	*Love Among The Ruins.*	Hartley: *The Go-Between.*
1955	Moves to a large country house in Somerset with his family. *Officers and Gentlemen*, the second part of the *Sword of Honour* trilogy.	Nabokov: *Lolita.* Miller: *A View from the Bridge.* Graham Greene: *Loser Takes All; The Quiet American.* Murdoch: *Under The Net.*
1956		Beckett: *Molloy.* Camus: *The Fall.* Faulkner: *Requiem for a Nun.*
1957	*The Ordeal of Gilbert Pinfold.*	Camus: *L'Exil et le Royaume.* Pasternak: *Doctor Zhivago.* Pinter: *The Birthday Party.* Nabokov: *Pnin.* Spark: *The Comforters.*
1959	Publishes a biography of Ronald Knox.	Spark: *Memento Mori.* Eliot: *The Elder Statesman.* Graham Greene: *The Complaisant Lover.* Beckett: *Endgame.*
1960	*A Tourist in Africa.*	Spark: *The Ballad of Peckham Rye.* Updike: *Rabbit, Run.* Pinter: *The Caretaker.* Betjeman: *Summoned by Bells.*
1961	*Unconditional Surrender*, the final part of the *Sword of Honour* trilogy.	Graham Greene: *A Burnt-Out Case.* Albee: *The American Dream.* Huxley: *Religion without Revelation.* Spark: *The Prime of Miss Jean Brodie.*
1962	*Tactical Exercise.*	Albee: *Who's Afraid of Virginia Woolf?* Isherwood: *Down there on a Visit.*
1963	*Basil Seal Rides Again.*	Stoppard: *A Walk on Water.* Pinter: *The Lover.* Spark: *The Girls of Slender Means.*
1964	*A Little Learning*, an autobiography.	Sartre: *Les Mots.* Ayme: *The Minotaur.* Isherwood: *A Single Man.*
1965		Pinter: *The Homecoming.* Albee: *Tiny Alice.*
1966	Waugh dies at his home after Mass on Easter Sunday.	Albee: *A Delicate Balance.*

CHRONOLOGY

Burgess and Maclean defect to USSR.

Josef Stalin dies. USSR anti-Semite campaign.
USSR denounces its alliances with France and Britain. West Germany joins NATO.

Suez crisis and invasion of Hungary by USSR.

Macmillan becomes Prime Minister. Adenauer obtains an absolute majority in German elections. Gromyko becomes Minister for foreign affairs in the USSR. Suez canal re-opened.

De Gaulle becomes President of the French Republic. Castro becomes the leader of Cuba.

J. F. Kennedy becomes US President.

Khrushchev in UNO leads to a public scandal. Cuban missile crisis. Berlin wall is constructed. Britain applies to join the Common Market.

Spiegel affair in East Germany. Anglo-French agreement on the construction of Concorde.

Assassination of President Kennedy. Profumo affair. Douglas-Home becomes Prime Minister. Britain joins the Common Market.

Wilson becomes Prime Minister. Martin Luther King is awarded the Nobel Peace prize.

To
HAROLD ACTON
*in Homage and
Affection*

CONTENTS

CONTENTS

PART THREE

PRELUDE

MR SNIGGS, the Junior Dean, and Mr Postlethwaite, the Domestic Bursar, sat alone in Mr Sniggs' room overlooking the garden quad at Scone College. From the rooms of Sir Alastair Digby-Vane-Trumpington, two staircases away, came a confused roaring and breaking of glass. They alone of the senior members of Scone were at home that evening, for it was the night of the annual dinner of the Bollinger Club. The others were all scattered over Boar's Hill and North Oxford at gay, contentious little parties, or at other senior common-rooms, or at the meetings of learned societies, for the annual Bollinger dinner is a difficult time for those in authority.

It is not accurate to call this an annual event, because quite often the Club is suspended for some years after each meeting. There is tradition behind the Bollinger; it numbers reigning kings among its past members. At the last dinner, three years ago, a fox had been brought in in a cage and stoned to death with champagne bottles. What an evening that had been! This was the first meeting since then, and from all over Europe old members had rallied for the occasion. For two days they had been pouring into Oxford: epileptic royalty from their villas of exile; uncouth peers from crumbling country seats; smooth young men of uncertain tastes from embassies and legations; illiterate lairds from wet granite hovels in the Highlands; ambitious young barristers and Conservative candidates torn from the London season and the indelicate advances of debutantes; all that was most sonorous of name and title was there for the beano.

'The fines!' said Mr Sniggs, gently rubbing his pipe along the side of his nose. 'Oh my! the fines there'll be after this evening!'

3

There is some highly prized port in the senior common-room cellars that is only brought up when the College fines have reached £50.

'We shall have a week of it at least,' said Mr Postlethwaite, 'a week of Founder's port.'

A shriller note could now be heard rising from Sir Alastair's rooms; any who have heard that sound will shrink at the recollection of it; it is the sound of the English county families baying for broken glass. Soon they would all be tumbling out into the quad, crimson and roaring in their bottle-green evening coats, for the real romp of the evening.

'Don't you think it might be wiser if we turned out the light?' said Mr Sniggs.

In darkness the two dons crept to the window. The quad below was a kaleidoscope of dimly discernible faces.

'There must be fifty of them at least,' said Mr Postlethwaite. 'If only they were all members of the College! Fifty of them at ten pounds each. Oh my!'

'It'll be more if they attack the Chapel,' said Mr Sniggs. 'Oh, please God, make them attack the Chapel.'

'I wonder who the unpopular undergraduates are this term. They always attack their rooms. I hope they have been wise enough to go out for the evening.'

'I think Partridge will be one; he possesses a painting by Matisse or some such name.'

'And I'm told he has black sheets on his bed.'

'And Sanders went to dinner with Ramsay MacDonald once.'

'And Rending can afford to hunt, but collects china instead.'

'And smokes cigars in the garden after breakfast.'

'Austen has a grand piano.'

'They'll enjoy smashing that.'

'There'll be a heavy bill for to-night; just you see! But I confess I should feel easier if the Dean or the Master were in. They can't see us from here, can they?'

It was a lovely evening. They broke up Mr Austen's grand piano, and stamped Lord Rending's cigars into his carpet, and

smashed his china, and tore up Mr Partridge's sheets, and
threw the Matisse into his water-jug; Mr Sanders had nothing
to break except his windows, but they found the manuscript
at which he had been working for the Newdigate Prize Poem,
and had great fun with that. Sir Alastair Digby-Vane-
Trumpington felt quite ill with excitement, and was supported to bed by Lumsden of Strathdrummond. It was half-past
eleven. Soon the evening would come to an end. But there
was still a treat to come.

*

Paul Pennyfeather was reading for the Church. It was his third
year of uneventful residence at Scone. He had come there after
a creditable career at a small public school of ecclesiastical
temper on the South Downs, where he had edited the maga-
zine, been President of the Debating Society, and had, as his
report said, 'exercised a wholesome influence for good' in the
House in which he was head boy. At home he lived in Onslow
Square with his guardian, a prosperous solicitor who was proud
of his progress and abysmally bored by his company. Both
his parents had died in India at the time when he won the
essay prize at his preparatory school. For two years he had
lived within his allowance, aided by two valuable scholarships.
He smoked three ounces of tobacco a week – John Cotton,
Medium – and drank a pint and a half of beer a day, the half
at luncheon and the pint at dinner, a meal he invariably
ate in Hall. He had four friends, three of whom had been at
school with him. None of the Bollinger Club had ever heard
of Paul Pennyfeather, and he, oddly enough, had not heard of
them.

Little suspecting the incalculable consequences that the
evening was to have for him, he bicycled happily back from a
meeting of the League of Nations Union. There had been a
most interesting paper about plebiscites in Poland. He thought
of smoking a pipe and reading another chapter of the *Forsyte
Saga* before going to bed. He knocked at the gate, was

admitted, put away his bicycle, and diffidently, as always, made his way across the quad towards his rooms. What a lot of people there seemed to be about! Paul had no particular objection to drunkenness – he had read a rather daring paper to the Thomas More Society on the subject – but he was consumedly shy of drunkards.

Out of the night Lumsden of Strathdrummond swayed across his path like a druidical rocking-stone. Paul tried to pass.

Now it so happened that the tie of Paul's old school bore a marked resemblance to the pale blue and white of the Bollinger Club. The difference of a quarter of an inch in the width of the stripes was not one that Lumsden of Strathdrummond was likely to appreciate.

'Here's an awful man wearing the Boller tie,' said the Laird. It is not for nothing that since pre-Christian times his family had exercised chieftainship over unchartered miles of barren moorland.

Mr Sniggs was looking rather apprehensively at Mr Postlethwaite.

'They appear to have caught somebody,' he said. 'I hope they don't do him any serious harm.'

'Dear me, can it be Lord Reading? I think I ought to intervene.'

'No, Sniggs,' said Mr Postlethwaite, laying a hand on his impetuous colleague's arm. 'No, no, no. It would be unwise. We have the prestige of the senior common-room to consider. In their present state they might not prove amenable to discipline. We must at all costs avoid an *outrage*.'

At length the crowd parted, and Mr Sniggs gave a sigh of relief.

'But it's quite all right. It isn't Reading. It's Pennyfeather – someone of no importance.'

'Well, that saves a great deal of trouble. I am glad, Sniggs; I am, really. What a lot of clothes the young man appears to have lost!'

*

Next morning there was a lovely College meeting.

'Two hundred and thirty pounds,' murmured the Domestic Bursar ecstatically, '*not* counting the damage! That means five evenings, with what we have already collected. Five evenings of Founder's port!'

'The case of Pennyfeather,' the Master was saying, 'seems to be quite a different matter altogether. He ran the whole length of the quadrangle, you say, *without his trousers*. It is unseemly. It is more: it is indecent. In fact, I am almost prepared to say that it is flagrantly indecent. It is *not* the conduct we expect of a scholar.'

'Perhaps if we fined him really heavily?' suggested the Junior Dean.

'I very much doubt whether he could pay. I understand he is not well off. *Without trousers*, indeed! And at that time of night! I think we should do far better to get rid of him altogether. That sort of young man does the College no good.'

*

Two hours later, while Paul was packing his three suits in his little leather trunk, the Domestic Bursar sent a message that he wished to see him.

'Ah, Mr Pennyfeather,' he said, 'I have examined your rooms and noticed two slight burns, one on the windowsill and the other on the chimneypiece, no doubt from cigarette ends. I am charging you five-and-sixpence for each of them on your battels. That is all, thank you.'

As he crossed the quad Paul met Mr Sniggs.

'Just off?' said the Junior Dean brightly.

'Yes, sir,' said Paul.

And a little farther on he met the Chaplain.

'Oh, Pennyfeather, before you go, surely you have my copy of Dean Stanley's *Eastern Church*?'

'Yes. I left it on your table.'

'Thank you. Well, good-bye, my dear boy. I suppose that after that reprehensible affair last night you will have to think of some other profession. Well, you may congratulate yourself that you discovered your unfitness for the priesthood before it was too late. If a parson does a thing of that sort, you know, all the world knows. And so many do, alas! What do you propose doing?'

'I don't really know yet.'

'There is always commerce, of course. Perhaps you may be able to bring to the great world of business some of the ideals you have learned at Scone. But it won't be easy, you know. It is a thing to be lived down with courage. What did Dr Johnson say about fortitude? ... Dear, dear! *no trousers!*'

At the gates Paul tipped the porter.

'Well, good-bye, Blackall,' he said. 'I don't suppose I shall see you again for some time.'

'No, sir, and very sorry I am to hear about it. I expect you'll be becoming a schoolmaster, sir. That's what most of the gentlemen does, sir, that gets sent down for indecent behaviour.'

'God damn and blast them all to hell,' said Paul meekly to himself as he drove to the station, and then he felt rather ashamed, because he rarely swore.

PART ONE

CHAPTER I
Vocation

'SENT down for indecent behaviour, eh?' said Paul Penny-feather's guardian. 'Well, thank God your poor father has been spared this disgrace. That's all I can say.'

There was a hush in Onslow Square, unbroken except by Paul's guardian's daughter's gramophone playing Gilbert and Sullivan in her little pink boudoir at the top of the stairs.

'My daughter must know nothing of this,' continued Paul's guardian.

There was another pause.

'Well,' he resumed, 'you know the terms of your father's will. He left the sum of five thousand pounds, the interest of which was to be devoted to your education and the sum to be absolutely yours on your twenty-first birthday. That, if I am right, falls in eleven months' time. In the event of your education being finished before that time, he left me with complete discretion to withhold this allowance should I not consider your course of life satisfactory. I do not think that I should be fulfilling the trust which your poor father placed in me if, in the present circumstances, I continued any allowance. Moreover, you will be the first to realize how impossible it would be for me to ask you to share the same home with my daughter.'

'But what is to happen to me?' said Paul.

'I think you ought to find some work,' said his guardian thoughtfully. 'Nothing like it for taking the mind off nasty subjects.'

'But what kind of work?'

'Just work, good healthy toil. You have led too sheltered a life, Paul. Perhaps I am to blame. It will do you the world of good to face facts a bit – look at life in the raw, you know. See things steadily and see them whole, eh?' And Paul's guardian lit another cigar.

'Have I no legal right to any money at all?' asked Paul.

'None whatever, my dear boy,' said his guardian quite cheerfully. . . .

That spring Paul's guardian's daughter had two new evening frocks and, thus glorified, became engaged to a well-conducted young man in the Office of Works.

*

'Sent down for indecent behaviour, eh?' said Mr Levy, of Church and Gargoyle, scholastic agents. 'Well, I don't think we'll say anything about that. In fact, officially, mind, you haven't told me. We call that sort of thing "Education discontinued for personal reasons", you understand.' He picked up the telephone. 'Mr Samson, have we any "education discontinued" posts, male, on hand? . . . Right! . . . Bring it up, will you? I think,' he added, turning again to Paul, 'we have just the thing for you.'

A young man brought in a slip of paper.

'What about that?'

Paul read it:

Private and Confidential Notice of Vacancy.

Augustus Fagan, Esquire, Ph.D., Llanabba Castle, N. Wales, requires immediately Junior assistant master to teach Classics and English to University Standard with subsidiary Mathematics, German and French. Experience essential; first-class games essential.

Status of School: *School.*

Salary offered: £120 *resident post.*

Reply promptly but carefully to Dr Fagan ('Esq., Ph.D.,' on envelope), enclosing copies of testimonials and photographs, if considered advisable, mentioning that you have heard of the vacancy through us.

'Might have been made for you,' said Mr Levy.

'But I don't know a word of German, I've had no experience, I've got no testimonials, and I can't play cricket.'

'It doesn't do to be too modest,' said Mr Levy. 'It's wonderful what one can teach when one tries. Why, only last term we sent a man who had never been in a laboratory in his life as senior Science Master to one of our leading public schools. He came wanting to do private coaching in music. He's doing very well, I believe. Besides, Dr Fagan can't expect *all* that for the salary he's offering. Between ourselves, Llanabba hasn't a good name in the profession. We class schools, you see, into four grades: Leading School, First-rate School, Good School, and School. Frankly,' said Mr Levy, 'school is pretty bad. I think you'll find it a very suitable post. So far as I know, there are only two other candidates, and one of them is totally deaf, poor fellow.'

*

Next day Paul went to Church and Gargoyle to interview Dr Fagan. He had not long to wait. Dr Fagan was already there interviewing the other candidates. After a few minutes Mr Levy led Paul into the room, introduced him, and left them together.

'A most exhausting interview,' said Dr Fagan. 'I am sure he was a very nice young man, but I could not make him understand a word I said. Can *you* hear me quite clearly?'

'Perfectly, thank you.'

'Good; then let us get to business.'

Paul eyed him shyly across the table. He was very tall and very old and very well dressed; he had sunken eyes and rather long white hair over jet black eyebrows. His head was very long, and swayed lightly as he spoke; his voice had a thousand modulations, as though at some remote time he had taken lessons in elocution; the backs of his hands were hairy, and his fingers were crooked like claws.

'I understand you have had no previous experience?'

'No, sir, I am afraid not.'

'Well, of course, that is in many ways an advantage. One too easily acquires the professional tone and loses vision. But

of course we must be practical. I am offering a salary of one
hundred and twenty pounds, but only to a man with experience. I have a letter here from a young man who holds a
diploma in forestry. He wants an extra ten pounds a year on
the strength of it, but it is vision I need, Mr Pennyfeather, not
diplomas. I understand, too, that you left your University
rather suddenly. Now – why was that?'

This was the question that Paul had been dreading, and,
true to his training, he had resolved upon honesty.

'I was sent down, sir, for indecent behaviour.'

'Indeed, indeed? Well, I shall not ask for details. I have
been in the scholastic profession long enough to know that
nobody enters it unless he has some very good reason which
he is anxious to conceal. But, again to be practical, Mr
Pennyfeather, I can hardly pay one hundred and twenty
pounds to anyone who has been sent down for indecent
behaviour. Suppose that we fix your salary at ninety pounds
a year to begin with? I have to return to Llanabba to-night.
There are six more weeks of term, you see, and I have lost a
master rather suddenly. I shall expect you to-morrow evening.
There is an excellent train from Euston that leaves at about
ten. I think you will like your work,' he continued dreamily,
'you will find that my school is built upon an ideal – an ideal
of service and fellowship. Many of the boys come from the
very best families. Little Lord Tangent has come to us this
term, the Earl of Circumference's son, you know. Such a nice
little chap, erratic, of course, like all his family, but he has
tone.' Dr Fagan gave a long sigh. 'I wish I could say the same
for my staff. Between ourselves, Pennyfeather, I think I shall
have to get rid of Grimes fairly soon. He is *not* out of the top
drawer, and boys notice these things. Now, your predecessor
was a thoroughly agreeable young man. I was sorry to lose
him. But he used to wake up my daughters coming back on
his motor bicycle at all hours of the night. He used to borrow
money from the boys, too, quite large sums, and the parents
objected. I had to get rid of him. . . . Still, I was very sorry.
He had tone.'

Dr Fagan rose, put on his hat at a jaunty angle, and drew on a glove.

'Good-bye, my dear Pennyfeather. I think, in fact I know, that we are going to work well together. I can always tell these things.'

'Good-bye, sir,' said Paul. . . .

'Five per cent of ninety pounds is four pounds ten shillings,' said Mr Levy cheerfully. 'You can pay now or on receipt of your first term's salary. If you pay now there is a reduction of 15 per cent. That would be three pounds six shillings and sixpence.'

'I'll pay you when I get my wages,' said Paul.

'Just as you please,' said Mr Levy. 'Only too glad to have been of use to you.'

CHAPTER II
Llanabba Castle

LLANABBA CASTLE presents two quite different aspects, according as you approach it from the Bangor or the coast road. From the back it looks very much like any other large country house, with a great many windows and a terrace, and a chain of glass-houses and the roofs of innumerable nondescript kitchen buildings, disappearing into the trees. But from the front – and that is how it is approached from Llanabba station – it is formidably feudal; one drives past at least a mile of machicolated wall before reaching the gates; these are towered and turreted and decorated with heraldic animals and a workable portcullis. Beyond them at the end of the avenue stands the Castle, a model of medieval impregnability.

The explanation of this rather striking contrast is simple enough. At the time of the cotton famine in the sixties Llanabba House was the property of a prosperous Lancashire millowner. His wife could not bear to think of their men starving; in fact, she and her daughters organized a little bazaar in their aid, though without any very substantial results. Her husband had read the Liberal economists and could not think of paying without due return. Accordingly 'enlightened self-interest' found a way. An encampment of mill-hands was settled in the park, and they were put to work walling the grounds and facing the house with great blocks of stone from a neighbouring quarry. At the end of the American war they returned to their mills, and Llanabba House became Llanabba Castle after a great deal of work had been done very cheaply.

Driving up from the station in a little closed taxi, Paul saw little of all this. It was almost dark in the avenue and quite dark inside the house.

'I am Mr Pennyfeather,' he said to the butler. 'I have come here as a master.'

'Yes,' said the butler, 'I know all about you. This way.'

They went down a number of passages, unlit and smelling obscurely of all the ghastly smells of school, until they reached a brightly lighted door.

'In there. That's the Common Room.' Without more ado, the butler made off into the darkness.

Paul looked round. It was not a very big room. Even he felt that, and all his life he had been accustomed to living in constricted spaces.

'I wonder how many people live here,' he thought, and with a sick thrust of apprehension counted sixteen pipes in a rack at the side of the chimneypiece. Two gowns hung on a hook behind the door. In a corner were some golf clubs, a walking stick, an umbrella, and two miniature rifles. Over the chimneypiece was a green baize notice-board covered with lists; there was a typewriter on the table. In a bookcase were a number of very old textbooks and some new exercise-books. There were also a bicycle pump, two armchairs, a straight chair, half a bottle of invalid port, a boxing-glove, a bowler hat, yesterday's *Daily News*, and a packet of pipe-cleaners.

Paul sat down disconsolately on the straight chair.

Presently there was a knock at the door, and a small boy came in.

'Oh!' he said, looking at Paul intently.

'Hullo!' said Paul.

'I was looking for Captain Grimes,' said the little boy.

'Oh!' said Paul.

The child continued to look at Paul with a penetrating, impersonal interest.

'I suppose you're the new master?' he said.

'Yes,' said Paul. 'I'm called Pennyfeather.'

The little boy gave a shrill laugh. 'I think that's terribly funny,' he said, and went away.

Presently the door opened again, and two more boys looked in. They stood and giggled for a time and then made off.

In the course of the next half hour six or seven boys appeared on various pretexts and stared at Paul.

Then a bell rang, and there was a terrific noise of whistling and scampering. The door opened, and a very short man of about thirty came into the Common Room. He had made a great deal of noise in coming because he had an artificial leg. He had a short red moustache, and was slightly bald.

'Hullo!' he said.

'Hullo!' said Paul.

'I'm Captain Grimes,' said the newcomer, and 'Come in, you,' he added to someone outside.

Another boy came in.

'What do you mean,' said Grimes, 'by whistling when I told you to stop?'

'Everyone else was whistling,' said the boy.

'What's that got to do with it?' said Grimes.

'I should think it had a lot to do with it,' said the boy.

'Well, just you do a hundred lines, and next time, remember, I shall beat you,' said Grimes, 'with this,' said Grimes, waving the walking-stick.

'That wouldn't hurt much,' said the boy, and went out.

'There's no discipline in the place,' said Grimes, and then he went out too.

'I wonder whether I'm going to enjoy being a schoolmaster,' thought Paul.

Quite soon another and older man came into the room.

'Hullo!' he said to Paul.

'Hullo!' said Paul.

'I'm Prendergast,' said the newcomer. 'Have some port?'

'Thank you, I'd love to.'

'Well, there's only one glass.'

'Oh, well, it doesn't matter, then.'

'You might get your tooth-glass from your bedroom.'

'I don't know where that is.'

'Oh, well, never mind; we'll have some another night. I suppose you're the new master?'

'Yes.'

'You'll hate it here. I know. I've been here ten years. Grimes only came this term. He hates it already. Have you seen Grimes?'

'Yes, I think so.'

'He isn't a gentleman. Do you smoke?'

'Yes.'

'A pipe, I mean.'

'Yes.'

'Those are my pipes. Remind me to show them to you after dinner.'

At this moment the butler appeared with a message that Dr Fagan wished to see Mr Pennyfeather.

Dr Fagan's part of the Castle was more palatial. He stood at the end of a long room with his back to a rococo marble chimneypiece; he wore a velvet dinner-jacket.

'Settling in?' he asked.

'Yes,' said Paul.

Sitting before the fire, with a glass bottle of sweets in her lap, was a brightly dressed woman in early middle age.

'That,' said Dr Fagan with some disgust, 'is my daughter.'

'Pleased to meet you,' said Miss Fagan. 'Now what I always tells the young chaps as comes here is, "Don't let the dad overwork you." He's a regular Tartar, is Dad, but then you know what scholars are – inhuman. Ain't you,' said Miss Fagan, turning on her father with sudden ferocity – 'ain't you inhuman?'

'At times, my dear, I am grateful for what little detachment I have achieved. But here,' he added, 'is my other daughter.'

Silently, except for a scarcely perceptible jingling of keys, another woman had entered the room. She was younger than her sister, but far less gay.

'How do you do?' she said. 'I do hope you have brought some soap with you. I asked my father to tell you, but he so often forgets these things. Masters are not supplied with soap or with boot polish or with washing over two shillings and sixpence weekly. Do you take sugar in your tea?'

'Yes, usually.'

'I will make a note of that and have two extra lumps put out for you. Don't let the boys get them, though.'

'I have put you in charge of the fifth form for the rest of this term,' said Dr Fagan. 'You will find them delightful boys, quite delightful. Clutterbuck wants watching, by the way, a very delicate little chap. I have also put you in charge of the games, the carpentering class, and the fire drill. And I forgot, do you teach music?'

'No, I'm afraid not.'

'Unfortunate, most unfortunate. I understood from Mr Levy that you did. I have arranged for you to take Beste-Chetwynde in organ lessons twice a week. Well, you must do the best you can. There goes the bell for dinner. I won't detain you. Oh, one other thing. Not a word to the boys, please, about the reasons for your leaving Oxford! We schoolmasters must temper discretion with deceit. There, I fancy I have said something for you to think about. Good night.'

'Tootle-oo,' said the elder Miss Fagan.

CHAPTER III
Captain Grimes

PAUL had very little difficulty in finding the dining-hall. He was guided there by the smell of cooking and the sound of voices. It was a large, panelled room, far from disagreeable, with fifty or sixty boys of ages ranging from ten to eighteen settled along four long tables. The smaller ones wore Eton suits, the elder ones dinner-jackets.

He was led to a place at the head of one of the tables. The boys on either side of him stood up very politely until he sat down. One of them was the boy who had whistled at Captain Grimes. Paul thought he rather liked him.

'I'm called Beste-Chetwynde,' he said.

'I've got to teach you the organ, I believe.'

'Yes, it's great fun: we play in the village church. Do you play terribly well?'

Paul felt this was not a moment for candour, and so, 'tempering discretion with deceit', he said, 'Yes, remarkably well.'

'I say, do you really, or are you rotting?'

'Indeed, I'm not. I used to give lessons to the Master of Scone.'

'Well, you won't be able to teach me much,' said Beste-Chetwynde cheerfully. 'I only do it to get off gym. I say, they haven't given you a napkin. These servants are too awful. Philbrick,' he shouted to the butler, 'why haven't you given Mr Pennyfeather a napkin?'

'Forgot,' said Philbrick, 'and it's too late because Miss Fagan's locked the linen up.'

'Nonsense!' said Beste-Chetwynde; 'go and get one at once. That man's all right, really,' he added, 'only he wants watching.'

In a few minutes Philbrick returned with the napkin.

'It seems to me that you're a remarkably intelligent boy,' said Paul.

'Captain Grimes doesn't think so. He says I'm halfwitted. I'm glad you're not like Captain Grimes. He's so common, don't you think?'

'You mustn't talk about the other masters like that in front of me.'

'Well that's what we all think about him, anyway. What's more, he wears combinations. I saw it in his washing-book one day when I was fetching him his hat. I think combinations are rather awful, don't you?'

There was a commotion at the end of the hall.

'I expect that's Clutterbuck being sick,' said Beste-Chetwynde. 'He's awfully sick when we have mutton.'

The boy on Paul's other side now spoke for the first time.

'Mr Prendergast wears a wig,' he said, and then became very confused and subsided into a giggle.

'That's Briggs,' said Beste-Chetwynde, 'only everyone calls him Brolly, because of the shop, you know.'

'They're silly rotters,' said Briggs.

All this was a great deal easier than Paul had expected; it didn't seem so very hard to get on with boys, after all.

After a time they all stood up, and amid considerable noise Mr Prendergast said grace. Someone called out 'Prendy!' very loudly just by Paul's ear.

'. . . *per Christum Dominum nostrum. Amen*,' said Mr Prendergast. 'Beste-Chetwynde, was that you who made that noise?'

'Me, sir? No, sir.'

'Pennyfeather, did Beste-Chetwynde make that noise?'

'No, I don't think so,' said Paul, and Beste-Chetwynde gave him a friendly look, because, as a matter of fact, he had.

Captain Grimes linked arms with him outside the dining-hall.

'Filthy meal, isn't it, old boy?' he said.

'Pretty bad,' said Paul.

'Prendy's on duty to-night. I'm off to the pub. How about you?'

'All right,' said Paul.

'Prendy's not so bad in his way,' said Grimes, 'but he can't keep order. Of course, you know he wears a wig. Very hard for a man with a wig to keep order. I've got a false leg, but that's different. Boys respect that. Think I lost it in the war. Actually,' said the Captain, 'and strictly between ourselves, mind, I was run over by a tram in Stoke-on-Trent when I was one-over-the-eight. Still, it doesn't do to let that out to everyone. Funny thing, but I feel I can trust you. I think we're going to be pals.'

'I hope so,' said Paul.

'I've been feeling the need of a pal for some time. The bloke before you wasn't bad – a bit stand-offish, though. He had a motor-bike, you see. The daughters of the house didn't care for him. Have you met Miss Fagan?'

'I've met two.'

'They're both bitches,' said Grimes, and added moodily, 'I'm engaged to be married to Flossie.'

'Good God! Which is she?'

'The elder. The boys call them Flossie and Dingy. We haven't told the old boy yet. I'm waiting till I land in the soup again. Then I shall play that as my last card. I generally get into the soup sooner or later. Here's the pub. Not such a bad little place in its way. Clutterbuck's father makes all the beer round here. Not bad stuff, either. Two pints, please, Mrs Roberts!'

In the farther corner sat Philbrick, talking volubly in Welsh to a shady-looking old man.

'Damned cheek his coming in here!' said Grimes.

Mrs Roberts brought them their beer. Grimes took a long draught and sighed happily.

'This looks like being the first end of term I've seen for two years,' he said dreamily. 'Funny thing, I can always get on all right for about six weeks, and then I land in the soup. I don't believe I was ever meant by Nature to be a schoolmaster. Temperament,' said Grimes, with a far-away look in his eyes – 'that's been my trouble, temperament and sex.'

'Is it quite easy to get another job after – after you've been in the soup?' asked Paul.

'Not at first, it isn't, but there're ways. Besides, you see, I'm a public school man. That means everything. There's a blessed equity in the English social system,' said Grimes, 'that ensures the public school man against starvation. One goes through four or five years of perfect hell at an age when life is bound to be hell, anyway, and after that the social system never lets one down.

'Not that I stood four or five years of it, mind; I got the push soon after my sixteenth birthday. But my housemaster was a public school man. He knew the system. "Grimes," he said, "I can't keep you in the House after what has happened. I have the other boys to consider. But I don't want to be too hard on you. I want you to start again." So he sat down there and then and wrote me a letter of recommendation to any future employer, a corking good letter, too. I've got it still. It's been very useful at one time or another. That's the public school system all over. They may kick you out, but they never let you down.

'I subscribed a guinea to the War Memorial Fund. I felt I owed it to them. I was really sorry,' said Grimes, 'that that cheque never got through.

'After that I went into business. Uncle of mine had a brush factory at Edmonton. Doing pretty well before the war. That put the lid on the brush trade for me. You're too young to have been in the war, I suppose? Those were days, old boy. We shan't see the like of them again. I don't suppose I was really sober for more than a few hours for the whole of that war. Then I got into the soup again, pretty badly that time. Happened over in France. They said, "Now, Grimes, you've got to behave like a gentleman. We don't want a court-martial in this regiment. We're going to leave you alone for half an hour. There's your revolver. You know what to do. Good-bye, old man," they said quite affectionately.

'Well, I sat there for some time looking at that revolver. I put it up to my head twice, but each time I brought it down again. "Public school men don't end like this," I said to myself. It was a long half hour, but luckily they had left a decanter of whisky in there with me. They'd all had a few, I think. That's what made them all so solemn. There wasn't much whisky left when they came back, and, what with that and the strain of the situation, I could only laugh when they came in. Silly thing to do, but they looked so surprised, seeing me there alive and drunk.

' "The man's a cad," said the colonel, but even then I couldn't stop laughing, so they put me under arrest and called a court-martial.

'I must say I felt pretty low next day. A major came over from another battalion to try my case. He came to see me first, and bless me if it wasn't a cove I'd known at school.

' "God bless my soul," he said, "if it isn't Grimes of Podger's! What's all this nonsense about a court-martial?" So I told him. "H'm," he said, "pretty bad. Still, it's out of the question to shoot an old Harrovian. I'll see what I can do about it." And next day I was sent to Ireland on a pretty cushy job connected with postal service. That saw me out as far as the war was concerned. You can't get into the soup in Ireland, do what you like. I don't know if all this bores you?'

'Not at all,' said Paul. 'I think it's most encouraging.'

'I've been in the soup pretty often since then, but never quite so badly. Someone always turns up and says, "I can't see a public school man down and out. Let me put you on your feet again." I should think,' said Grimes, 'I've been put on my feet more often than any living man.'

Philbrick came across the bar parlour towards them.

'Feeling lonely?' he said. 'I've been talking to the station-master here, and if either of you wants an introduction to a young lady – '

'Certainly not,' said Paul.

'Oh, all right,' said Philbrick, making off.

'Women are an enigma,' said Grimes, 'as far as Grimes is concerned.'

CHAPTER IV
Mr Prendergast

PAUL was awakened next morning by a loud bang on his door, and Beste-Chetwynde looked in. He was wearing a very expensive-looking Charvat dressing-gown.

'Good morning, sir,' he said. 'I thought I'd come and tell you, as you wouldn't know: there's only one bathroom for the masters. If you want to get there before Mr Prendergast, you ought to go now. Captain Grimes doesn't wash much,' he added, and then disappeared.

Paul went to the bath and was rewarded some minutes later by hearing the shuffling of slippers down the passage and the door furiously rattled.

As he was dressing Philbrick appeared.

'Oh, I forgot to call you. Breakfast is in ten minutes.'

After breakfast Paul went up to the Common Room.

Mr Prendergast was there polishing his pipes, one by one, with a chamois leather. He looked reproachfully at Paul.

'We must come to some arrangement about the bathroom,' he said. 'Grimes very rarely has a bath. I have one before breakfast.'

'So do I,' said Paul defiantly.

'Then I suppose I shall have to find some other time,' said Mr Prendergast, and he gave a deep sigh as he returned his attention to his pipes. 'After ten years, too,' he added, 'but everything's like that. I might have known you'd want the bath. It was so easy when there was only Grimes and that other young man. He was never down in time for breakfast. Oh dear! oh dear! I can see that things are going to be very difficult.'

'But surely we could both have one?'

'No, no, that's out of the question. It's all part of the same thing. Everything has been like this since I left the ministry.'

Paul made no answer, and Mr Prendergast went on breathing and rubbing.

'I expect you wonder how I came to be here?'

23

'No, no,' said Paul soothingly. 'I think it's very natural.'

'It's not natural at all; it's most unnatural. If things had happened a little differently I should be a rector with my own little house and bathroom. I might even have been a rural dean, only' – and Mr Prendergast dropped his voice to a whisper – 'only I had *Doubts*.

'I don't know why I'm telling you all this, nobody else knows. I somehow feel you'll understand.

'Ten years ago I was a clergyman of the Church of England. I had just been presented to a living in Worthing. It was such an attractive church, not old, but *very* beautifully decorated, six candles on the altar, Reservation in the Lady Chapel, and an excellent heating apparatus which burned coke in a little shed by the sacristy door, no graveyard, just a hedge of golden privet between the church and the rectory.

'As soon as I moved in my mother came to keep house for me. She bought some chintz, out of her own money, for the drawing-room curtains. She used to be "at home" once a week to the ladies of the congregation. One of them, the dentist's wife, gave me a set of the *Encyclopaedia Britannica* for my study. It was all very pleasant until my *Doubts* began.'

'Were they as bad as all that?' asked Paul.

'They were insuperable,' said Mr Prendergast; 'that is why I am here now. But I expect I am boring you?'

'No, do go on. That's to say, unless you find it painful to think about.'

'I think about it all the time. It happened like this, quite suddenly. We had been there about three months, and my mother had made great friends with some people called Bundle – rather a curious name. I think he was an insurance agent until he retired. Mrs Bundle used very kindly to ask us in to supper on Sundays after Evensong. They were pleasant informal gatherings, and I used quite to look forward to them. I can see them now as they sat there on this particular evening; there was my mother and Mr and Mrs Bundle, and their son, rather a spotty boy, I remember, who used to go in to Brighton College by train every day, and Mrs Bundle's mother, a Mrs

Crump, rather deaf, but a very good Churchwoman, and Mrs Aber – that was the name of the dentist's wife who gave me the *Encyclopaedia Britannica* – and old Major Ending, the people's warden. I had preached two sermons that day besides taking the children's Bible-class in the afternoon, and I had rather dropped out of the conversation. They were all talking away quite happily about the preparations that were being made on the pier for the summer season, when suddenly, for no reason at all, my *Doubts* began.' He paused, and Paul felt constrained to offer some expression of sympathy.

'What a terrible thing!' he said.

'Yes, I've not known an hour's real happiness since. You see, it wasn't the ordinary sort of Doubt about Cain's wife or the Old Testament miracles or the consecration of Archbishop Parker. I'd been taught how to explain all those while I was at college. No, it was something deeper than all that. *I couldn't understand why God had made the world at all.* There was my mother and the Bundles and Mrs Crump talking away quite uncon-cernedly while I sat there wrestling with this sudden assault of doubt. You see how fundamental that is. Once granted the first step, I can see that everything else follows – Tower of Babel, Babylonian captivity, Incarnation, Church, bishops, in-cense, everything – but what I couldn't see, and what I can't see now, is, *why* did it all begin?'

'I asked my bishop; he didn't know. He said that he didn't think the point really arose as far as my practical duties as a parish priest were concerned. I discussed it with my mother. At first she was inclined to regard it as a passing phase. But it didn't pass, so finally she agreed with me that the only honourable thing to do was to resign my living; she never really recovered from the shock, poor old lady. It was a great blow after she had bought the chintz and got so friendly with the Bundles.'

A bell began ringing down a distant passage.

'Well, well, we must go to prayers, and I haven't finished my pipes.' He took his gown from the peg behind the door and slipped it over his shoulders.

'Perhaps one day I shall see Light,' he said, 'and then I shall go back to the ministry. Meanwhile –'

Clutterbuck ran past the door, whistling hideously.

'That's a nasty little boy,' said Mr Prendergast, 'if ever there was one.'

CHAPTER V
Discipline

PRAYERS were held downstairs in the main hall of the Castle. The boys stood ranged along the panelled walls, each holding in his hands a little pile of books. Grimes sat on one of the chairs beside the baronial chimneypiece.

'Morning,' he said to Paul; 'only just down, I'm afraid. Do I smell of drink?'

'Yes,' said Paul.

'Comes of missing breakfast. Prendy been telling you about his Doubts?'

'Yes,' said Paul.

'Funny thing,' said Grimes, 'but I've never been worried in that way. I don't pretend to be a particularly pious sort of chap, but I've never had any Doubts. When you've been in the soup as often as I have, it gives you a sort of feeling that everything's for the best, really. You know, God's in His heaven; all's right with the world. I can't quite explain it, but I don't believe one can ever be unhappy for long provided one does just exactly what one wants to and when one wants to. The last chap who put me on my feet said I was "singularly in harmony with the primitive promptings of humanity." I've remembered that phrase because somehow it seemed to fit me. Here comes the old man. This is where we stand up.'

As the bell stopped ringing Dr Fagan swept into the hall, the robes of a Doctor of Philosophy swelling and billowing about him. He wore an orchid in his buttonhole.

'Good morning, gentlemen,' he said.

'Good morning, sir,' chorused the boys.

The Doctor advanced to the table at the end of the room, picked up a Bible, and opening it at random, read a chapter of blood-curdling military history without any evident relish. From that he plunged into the Lord's prayer, which the boys took up in a quiet chatter. Prendergast's voice led them in tones that testified to his ecclesiastical past.

Then the Doctor glanced at a sheet of notes he held in his hand. 'Boys,' he said, 'I have some announcements to make. The Fagan cross-country running challenge cup will not be competed for this year on account of the floods.'

'I expect the old boy has popped it,' said Grimes in Paul's ear.

'Nor will the Llanabba Essay Prize.'

'On account of the floods,' said Grimes.

'I have received my account for the telephone,' proceeded Dr Fagan, 'and I find that during the past quarter there have been no less than twenty-three trunk calls to London, none of which was sent by me or by members of my family. I look to the prefects to stop this, unless of course they are themselves responsible, in which case I must urge them in my own interests to make use of the village post-office, to which they have access.

'I think that is everything, isn't it, Mr Prendergast?'

'*Cigars,*' said Mr Prendergast in a stage whisper.

'Ah yes, cigars. Boys, I have been deeply distressed to learn that several cigar ends have been found – where have they been found?'

'*Boiler-room.*'

'In the boiler-room. I regard this as reprehensible. What boy has been smoking cigars in the boiler-room?'

There was a prolonged silence, during which the Doctor's eye travelled down the line of boys.

'I will give the culprit until luncheon to give himself up. If I do not hear from him by then the whole school will be heavily punished.'

'Damn!' said Grimes. 'I gave those cigars to Clutterbuck. I hope the little beast has the sense to keep quiet.'

'Go to your classes,' said the Doctor.

The boys filed out.

'I should think, by the look of them, they were exceedingly cheap cigars,' added Mr Prendergast sadly. 'They were a pale yellow colour.'

'That makes it worse,' said the Doctor. 'To think of any boy under my charge smoking pale yellow cigars in a boiler-room! It is *not* a gentlemanly fault.'

The masters went upstairs.

'That's your little mob in there,' said Grimes; 'you let them out at eleven.'

'But what am I to teach them?' said Paul in sudden panic.

'Oh, I shouldn't try to *teach* them anything, not just yet, anyway. Just keep them quiet.'

'Now that's a thing I've never learned to do,' sighed Mr Prendergast.

Paul watched him amble into his classroom at the end of the passage, where a burst of applause greeted his arrival. Dumb with terror he went into his own classroom.

Ten boys sat before him, their hands folded, their eyes bright with expectation.

'Good morning, sir,' said the one nearest him.

'Good morning,' said Paul.

'Good morning, sir,' said the next.

'Good morning,' said Paul.

'Good morning, sir,' said the next.

'Oh, shut up,' said Paul.

At this the boy took out a handkerchief and began to cry quietly.

'Oh, sir,' came a chorus of reproach, 'you've hurt his feelings. He's very sensitive; it's his Welsh blood, you know; it makes people very emotional. Say "Good morning" to him, sir, or he won't be happy all day. After all, it is a good morning, isn't it, sir?'

'Silence!' shouted Paul above the uproar, and for a few moments things were quieter.

'Please, sir,' said a small voice – Paul turned and saw a grave-looking youth holding up his hand – 'please, sir, perhaps he's been smoking cigars and doesn't feel well.'

'Silence!' said Paul again.

The ten boys stopped talking and sat perfectly still staring at him. He felt himself getting hot and red under their scrutiny.

'I suppose the first thing I ought to do is to get your names clear. What is your name?' he asked, turning to the first boy.

'Tangent, sir.'

'And yours?'

'Tangent, sir,' said the next boy. Paul's heart sank.

'But you can't both be called Tangent.'

'No, sir, *I'm* Tangent. He's just trying to be funny.'

'I like that. *Me* trying to be funny! Please, sir, I'm Tangent, sir; really I am.'

'If it comes to that,' said Clutterbuck from the back of the room, 'there is only one Tangent here, and that is me. Anyone else can jolly well go to blazes.'

Paul felt desperate.

'Well, is there anyone who isn't Tangent?'

Four or five voices instantly arose.

'I'm not, sir; I'm not Tangent. I wouldn't be called Tangent, not on the end of a barge pole.'

In a few seconds the room had become divided into two parties: those who were Tangent and those who were not. Blows were already being exchanged, when the door opened and Grimes came in. There was a slight hush.

'I thought you might want this,' he said, handing Paul a walking-stick. 'And if you take my advice, you'll set them something to do.'

He went out; and Paul, firmly grasping the walking-stick, faced his form.

'Listen,' he said. 'I don't care a damn what any of you are called, but if there's another word from anyone I shall keep you all in this afternoon.'

'You can't keep me in,' said Clutterbuck; 'I'm going for a walk with Captain Grimes.'

'Then I shall very nearly kill you with this stick. Meanwhile you will all write an essay on "Self-indulgence". There will be a prize of half a crown for the longest essay, irrespective of any possible merit.'

From then onwards all was silence until break. Paul, still holding his stick, gazed despondently out of the window. Now and then there rose from below the shrill voices of the servants scolding each other in Welsh. By the time the bell rang Clutterbuck had covered sixteen pages, and was awarded the half-crown.

'Did you find those boys difficult to manage?' asked Mr Prendergast, filling his pipe.

'Not at all,' said Paul.

'Ah, you're lucky. I find all boys utterly intractable. I don't know why it is. Of course my wig has a lot to do with it. Have you noticed that I wear a wig?'

'No, no, of course not.'

'Well, the boys did as soon as they saw it. It was a great mistake my ever getting one. I thought when I left Worthing that I looked too old to get a job easily. I was only forty-one. It was very expensive, even though I chose the cheapest quality. Perhaps that's why it looks so like a wig. I don't know. I knew from the first that it was a mistake, but once they had seen it, it was too late to go back. They make all sorts of jokes about it.'

'I expect they'd laugh at something else if it wasn't that.'

'Yes, no doubt they would. I daresay it's a good thing to localize their ridicule as far as possible. Oh dear! oh dear! If it wasn't for my pipes, I don't know how I should manage to keep on. What made you come here?'

'I was sent down from Scone for indecent behaviour.'

'Oh yes, like Grimes?'

'No,' said Paul firmly, 'not like Grimes.'

'Oh, well, it's all much the same really. And there's the bell. Oh dear! oh dear! I believe that loathsome little man's taken my gown.'

*

Two days later Beste-Chetwynde pulled out the *vox humana* and played *Pop goes the Weasel*.

'D'you know, sir, you've made rather a hit with the fifth form?'

He and Paul were seated in the organ-loft of the village church. It was their second music-lesson.

'For goodness' sake, leave the organ alone. How d'you mean "hit"?'

'Well, Clutterbuck was in the matron's room this morning. He'd just got a tin of pineapple chunks. Tangent said, "Are you going to take that into Hall?" and he said, "No, I'm going to eat them in Mr Pennyfeather's hour." "Oh no, you're not," said Tangent. "Sweets and biscuits are one thing, but pineapple chunks are going too far. It's little stinkers like you," he said, "who turn decent masters savage." '

'Do you think that's so very complimentary?'

'I think it's one of the most complimentary things I ever heard said about a master,' said Beste-Chetwynde; 'would you like me to try that hymn again?'

'No,' said Paul decisively.

'Well, then, I'll tell you another thing,' said Beste-Chetwynde. 'You know that man Philbrick. Well, I think there's something odd about him.'

'I've no doubt of it.'

'It's not just that he's such a bad butler. The servants are always ghastly here. But I don't believe he's a butler at all.'

'I don't quite see what else he *can* be.'

'Well, have you ever known a butler with a diamond tie-pin?'

'No, I don't think I have.'

'Well, Philbrick's got one, and a diamond ring too. He showed them to Brolly. Colossal great diamonds, Brolly says. Philbrick said he used to have bushels of diamonds and emeralds before the war, and that he used to eat off gold plate. We believe that he's a Russian prince in exile.'

'Generally speaking, Russians are not shy about using their titles, are they? Besides, he looks very English.'

'Yes, we thought of that, but Brolly said lots of Russians came to school in England before the war. And now I *am* going to play the organ,' said Beste-Chetwynde. 'After all, my mother does pay five guineas a term extra for me to learn.'

CHAPTER VI
Conduct

SITTING over the Common Room fire that afternoon waiting for the bell for tea, Paul found himself reflecting that on the whole the last week had not been quite as awful as he had expected. As Beste-Chetwynde had told him, he was a distinct success with his form; after the first day an understanding had been established between them. It was tacitly agreed that when Paul wished to read or to write letters he was allowed to do so undisturbed while he left them to employ the time as they thought best; when Paul took it upon him to talk to them about their lessons they remained silent, and when he set them work to do some of it was done. It had rained steadily, so that there had been no games. No punishments, no reprisals, no exertion, and in the evenings the confessions of Grimes, any one of which would have glowed with outstanding shamelessness from the appendix to a treatise in psycho-analysis.

Mr Prendergast came in with the post.

'A letter for you, two for Grimes, nothing for me,' he said. 'No one ever writes to me. There was a time when I used to get five or six letters a day, not counting circulars. My mother used to file them for me to answer – one heap of charity appeals, another for personal letters, another for marriages and funerals, another for baptisms and churchings, and another for anonymous abuse. I wonder why it is the clergy always get so many letters of that sort, sometimes from quite educated people. I remember my father had great trouble in that way once, and he was forced to call in the police because they became so threatening. And, do you know, it was the curate's

wife who had sent them – such a quiet little woman. There's
your letter. Grimes' look like bills. I can't think why shops
give that man credit at all. I always pay cash, or at least I
should if I ever bought anything. But d'you know that, except
for my tobacco and the *Daily News* and occasionally a little
port when it's very cold, I don't think I've bought anything
for two years. The last thing I bought was that walking-stick.
I got it at Shanklin, and Grimes uses it for beating the
boys with. I hadn't really meant to buy one, but I was there
for the day – two years this August – and I went into the
tobacconist's to buy some tobacco. He hadn't the sort I wanted,
and I felt I couldn't go out without getting something, so I
bought that. It cost one-and-six,' he added wistfully, 'so I had
no tea.'

Paul took his letter. It had been forwarded from Onslow
Square. On the flap were embossed the arms of Scone College.
It was from one of his four friends.

> *Scone College, J.C.R.,*
> *Oxford.*

My dear Pennyfeather, it ran,

*I need hardly tell you how distressed I was when I heard of your
disastrous misfortune. It seems to me that a real injustice has been done
to you. I have not heard the full facts of the case, but I was confirmed
in my opinion by a very curious incident last evening. I was just going
to bed when Digby-Vane-Trumpington came into my rooms without
knocking. He was smoking a cigar. I had never spoken to him before, as
you know, and was very much surprised at his visit. He said: 'I'm told
you are a friend of Pennyfeather's.' I said I was, and he said: 'Well, I
gather I've rather got him into a mess'; I said: 'Yes,' and he said: 'Well,
will you apologize to him for me when you write?' I said I would. Then
he said: 'Look here, I'm told he's rather poor. I thought of sending him
some money – £20 for sort of damages, you know. It's all I can spare
at the moment. Wouldn't it be a useful thing to do?' I fairly let him
have it, I can tell you, and told him just what I thought of him for
making such an insulting suggestion. I asked him how he dared treat a
gentleman like that just because he wasn't in his awful set. He seemed*

rather taken aback and said: 'Well all my *friends spend all their time trying to get money out of me,' and went off.*

I bicycled over to St Magnus's at Little Bechley and took some rubbings of the brasses there. I wished you had been with me.

Yours,

Arthur Potts.

PS. – *I understand you are thinking of taking up educational work. It seems to me that the great problem of education is to train the moral perceptions, not merely to discipline the appetites. I cannot help thinking that it is in greater fastidiousness rather than in greater self-control that the future progress of the race lies. I shall be interested to hear what your experience has been over the matter. The chaplain does not agree with me in this. He says great sensibility usually leads to enervation of will. Let me know what you think.*

'What do you think about that?' asked Paul, handing Mr Prendergast the letter.

'Well,' he said after studying it carefully, 'I think your friend is wrong about sensibility. It doesn't do to rely on one's own feelings, does it, not in anything?'

'No, I mean about the money.'

'Good gracious, Pennyfeather! I hope you are in no doubt about that. Accept it at once, of course.'

'It's a temptation.'

'My dear boy, it would be a sin to refuse. Twenty pounds! Why, it takes me half a term to earn that.'

The bell rang for tea. In the dining-hall Paul gave the letter to Grimes.

'Shall I take the twenty pounds?' he asked.

'Take it? My God! I should think you would.'

'Well, I'm not sure,' said Paul.

He thought about it all through afternoon school, all the time he was dressing for dinner, and all through dinner. It was a severe struggle, but his early training was victorious.

'If I take that money,' he said to himself, 'I shall never know whether I have acted rightly or not. It would always be on my mind. If I refuse, I shall be sure of having done right. I shall look upon my self-denial with exquisite self-approval. By refusing I can convince myself that, in spite of the unbelievable things that have been happening to me during the last ten days, I am still the same Paul Pennyfeather I have respected so long. It is a test-case of the durability of my ideals.'

He tried to explain something of what he felt to Grimes as they sat in Mrs Roberts' bar parlour that evening.

'I'm afraid you'll find my attitude rather difficult to understand,' he said. 'I suppose it's largely a matter of upbringing. There is every reason why I should take this money. Digby-Vane-Trumpington is exceedingly rich; and if he keeps it, it will undoubtedly be spent on betting or on some deplorable debauch. Owing to his party I have suffered irreparable harm. My whole future is shattered, and I have directly lost one hundred and twenty pounds a year in scholarships and two hundred and fifty pounds a year allowance from my guardian. By any ordinary process of thought, the money is justly mine. But,' said Paul Pennyfeather, 'there is my honour. For generations the British bourgeoisie have spoken of themselves as gentlemen, and by that they have meant, among other things, a self-respecting scorn of irregular perquisites. It is the quality that distinguishes the gentleman from both the artist and the aristocrat. Now I am a gentleman. I can't help it: it's born in me. I just can't take that money.'

'Well, I'm a gentleman too, old boy,' said Grimes, 'and I was afraid you might feel like that, so I did my best for you and saved you from yourself.'

'What d'you mean by that?'

'Dear old boy, don't be angry, but immediately after tea I sent off a wire to your friend Potts: *Tell Trumpington send money quick*, and signed it "*Pennyfeather*". I don't mind lending you the bob till it comes, either.'

'Grimes, you wretch!' said Paul, but, in spite of himself, he felt a great wave of satisfaction surge up within him. 'We must have another drink on that.'

'Good for you,' said Grimes, 'and it's on me this round.'

'To the durability of ideals!' said Paul as he got his pint.

'My word, what a mouthful!' said Grimes; 'I can't say that. Cheerioh!'

*

Two days later came another letter from Arthur Potts:

Dear Pennyfeather,

I enclose Trumpington's cheque for £20. I am glad that my dealings with him are at an end. I cannot pretend to under-stand your attitude in this matter, but no doubt you are the best judge.

Stiggins is reading a paper to the O.S.C.U. on 'Sex Repression and Religious Experience'. *Everyone expects rather a row, because you know how keen Walton is on the mystical element, which I think Stiggins is inclined to discount.*

Yours,
Arthur Potts.

There is a most interesting article in the 'Educational Review' *on the new methods that are being tried at the Innesborough High School to induce co-ordination of the senses. They put small objects into the children's mouths and make them draw the shapes in red chalk. Have you tried this with your boys? I must say I envy you your opportunities. Are your colleagues enlightened?*

'This same Potts,' said Grimes as he read the letter, 'would appear to be something of a stinker. Still, we've got the doings. How about a binge?'

'Yes,' said Paul, 'I think we ought to do something about one. I should like to ask Prendy too.'

'Why, of course. It's just what Prendy needs. He's been looking awfully down in the mouth lately. Why shouldn't we all go over to the Metropole at Cwmpryddyg for dinner one night? We shall have to wait until the old boy goes away, otherwise he'll notice that there's no one on duty.'

Later in the day Paul suggested the plan to Mr Prendergast. 'Really, Pennyfeather,' he said, 'I think that's uncommonly kind of you. I hardly know what to say. Of course, I should love it. I can't remember when I dined at an hotel last. Certainly not since the war. It *will* be a treat. My dear boy. I'm quite overcome.'

And, much to Paul's embarrassment, a tear welled-up in each of Mr Prendergast's eyes, and coursed down his cheeks.

CHAPTER VII
Philbrick

THAT morning just before luncheon the weather began to show signs of clearing, and by half-past one the sun was shining. The Doctor made one of his rare visits to the school dining-hall. At his entry everybody stopped eating and laid down his knife and fork.

'Boys,' said the Doctor, regarding them benignly, 'I have an announcement to make. Clutterbuck, will you kindly stop eating while I am addressing the school. The boys' manners need correcting, Mr Prendergast. I look to the prefects to see to this. Boys, the chief sporting event of the year will take place in the playing-fields to-morrow. I refer to the Annual School Sports, unfortunately postponed last year owing to the General Strike. Mr Pennyfeather, who, as you know, is himself a distinguished athlete, will be in charge of all arrangements. The preliminary heats will be run off to-day. All boys must compete in all events. The Countess of Circumference has kindly consented to present the prizes. Mr Prendergast will act as referee, and Captain Grimes as timekeeper. I shall myself be present to-morrow to watch the final competitions. That is all, thank you. Mr Pennyfeather, perhaps you will favour me with an interview when you have finished your luncheon?'

'Good God!' murmured Paul.

'I won the long-jump at the last sports,' said Briggs, 'but everyone said that it was because I had spiked shoes. Do you wear spiked shoes, sir?'

'Invariably,' said Paul.

'Everyone said it was taking an unfair advantage. You see, we never know beforehand when there's going to be sports, so we don't have time to get ready.'

'My mamma's coming down to see me to-morrow,' said Beste-Chetwynde; 'just my luck! Now I shall have to stay here all the afternoon.'

After luncheon Paul went to the morning-room, where he found the Doctor pacing up and down in evident high excitement.

'Ah, come in, Pennyfeather! I am just making the arrangements for to-morrow's fête. Florence, will you get on to the Clutterbucks on the telephone and ask them to come over, and the Hope-Brownes. I think the Warringtons are too far away, but you might ask them, and of course the Vicar and old Major Sidebotham. The more guests the better, Florence!

'And, Diana, you must arrange the tea. Sandwiches, *foie gras* sandwiches – last time, you remember, the liver sausage you bought made Lady Bunyan ill – and cakes, plenty of cakes, with coloured sugar! You had better take the car into Llandudno and get them there.

'Philbrick, there must be champagne-cup, and will you help the men putting up the marquee. And flags, Diana! There must be flags left over from last time.'

'I made them into dusters,' said Dingy.

'Well, we must buy more. No expense must be spared. Pennyfeather, I want you to get the results of the first heats out by four o'clock. Then you can telephone them to the printers, and we shall have the programmes by to-morrow. Tell them that fifty will be enough; they must be decorated with the school colours and crest in gold. And there must be flowers, Diana, banks of flowers,' said the Doctor with an expansive gesture. 'The prizes shall stand among banks of flowers. Do you think there ought to be a bouquet for Lady Circumference?'

'No,' said Dingy.

'Nonsense!' said the Doctor. 'Of course there must be a bouquet. It is rarely that the scholarly calm of Llanabba gives place to festival, but when it does taste and dignity shall go unhampered. It shall be an enormous bouquet, redolent of hospitality. You are to produce the most expensive bouquet that Wales can offer; do you understand? Flowers, youth, wisdom, the glitter of jewels, music,' said the Doctor, his imagination soaring to dizzy heights under the stimulus of the words, 'music! There must be a band.'

'I never heard of such a thing,' said Dingy. 'A band indeed! You'll be having fireworks next.'

'*And fireworks*,' said the Doctor, 'and do you think it would be a good thing to buy Mr Prendergast a new tie? I noticed how shabby he looked this morning.'

'No,' said Dingy with finality, 'that is going too far. Flowers and fireworks are one thing, but I insist on drawing a line somewhere. It would be sinful to buy Mr Prendergast a tie.'

'Perhaps you are right,' said the Doctor. 'But there shall be music. I understand that the Llanabba Silver Band was third at the North Wales Eisteddfod last month. Will you get on to them, Florence? I think Mr Davies at the station is the bandmaster. Can the Clutterbucks come?'

'Yes,' said Flossie, 'six of them.'

'Admirable! And then there is the Press. We must ring up the *Flint and Denbigh Herald* and get them to send a photographer. That means whisky. Will you see to that, Philbrick? I remember at one of our sports I omitted to offer whisky to the Press, and the result was a *most* unfortunate photograph. Boys do get into such indelicate positions during the obstacle race, don't they?

'Then there are the prizes. I think you had better take Grimes into Llandudno with you to help with the prizes. I don't think there is any need for undue extravagance with the prizes. It gives boys a wrong idea of sport. I wonder whether Lady Circumference would think it odd if we asked her to present parsley crowns. Perhaps she would. Utility, economy, and apparent durability are the qualities to be sought for, I think.

'And, Pennyfeather, I hope you will see that they are distributed fairly evenly about the school. It doesn't do to let any boy win more than two events; I leave you to arrange that. I think it would be only right if little Lord Tangent won something, and Beste-Chetwynde – yes, his mother is coming down, too.

'I am afraid all this has been thrown upon your shoulders rather suddenly. I only learned this morning that Lady Circumference proposed to visit us, and as Mrs Beste-Chetwynde was coming too, it seemed too good an opportunity to be missed. It is not often that the visits of two such important parents coincide. She is the Honourable Mrs Beste-Chetwynde, you know – sister-in-law of Lord Pastmaster – a very wealthy woman, South American. They always say that she poisoned her husband, but of course little Beste-Chetwynde doesn't know that. It never came into court, but there was a great deal of talk about it at the time. Perhaps you remember the case?'

'No,' said Paul.

'Powdered glass,' said Flossie shrilly, 'in his coffee.'

'Turkish coffee,' said Dingy.

'To work!' said the Doctor; 'we have a lot to see to.'

*

It was raining again by the time that Paul and Mr Prendergast reached the playing-fields. The boys were waiting for them in bleak little groups, shivering at the unaccustomed austerity of bare knees and open necks. Clutterbuck had fallen down in the mud and was crying quietly behind a tree.

'How shall we divide them?' said Paul.

'I don't know,' said Mr Prendergast. 'Frankly, I deplore the whole business.'

Philbrick appeared in an overcoat and a bowler hat.

'Miss Fagan says she's very sorry, but she's burnt the hurdles and the jumping posts for firewood. She thinks she can hire some in Llandudno for to-morrow. The Doctor says you must do the best you can till then. I've got to help the gardeners put up the blasted tent.'

'I think that, if anything, sports are rather worse than concerts,' said Mr Prendergast. 'They at least happen indoors. Oh dear! oh dear! How wet I am getting. I should have got my boots mended if I'd known this was going to happen.'

'Please, sir,' said Beste-Chetwynde, 'we're all getting rather cold. Can we start?'

'Yes, I suppose so,' said Paul. 'What do you want to do?'

'Well, we ought to divide up into heats and then run a race.'

'All right! Get into four groups.'

This took some time. They tried to induce Mr Prendergast to run too.

'The first race will be a mile. Prendy, will you look after them? I want to see if Philbrick and I can fix up anything for the jumping.'

'But what am I to do?' said Mr Prendergast.

'Just make each group run to the Castle and back and take the names of the first two in each heat. It's quite simple.'

'I'll try,' he said sadly.

Paul and Philbrick went into the pavilion together.

'Me, a butler,' said Philbrick, 'made to put up tents like a blinking Arab!'

'Well, it's a change,' said Paul.

'It's a change for me to be a butler,' said Philbrick. 'I wasn't made to be anyone's servant.'

'No, I suppose not.'

'I expect you wonder how it is that I come to be here?' said Philbrick.

'No,' said Paul firmly, 'nothing of the kind. I don't in the least want to know anything about you; d'you hear?'

'I'll tell you,' said Philbrick; 'it was like this – '

'I don't want to hear your loathsome confessions; can't you understand?'

'It isn't a loathsome confession,' said Philbrick. 'It's a story of love. I think it is without exception the most beautiful story I know.

'I daresay you have heard of Sir Solomon Philbrick?'

'No,' said Paul.

'What, never heard of old Solly Philbrick?'

'No; why?'

'Because that's me. And I can tell you this. It's a pretty well-known name across the river. You've only to say Solly Philbrick, of the "Lamb and Flag", anywhere south of Waterloo Bridge to see what fame is. Try it.'

'I will one day.'

'Mind you, when I say *Sir* Solomon Philbrick, that's only a bit of fun, see? That's what the boys call me. Plain Mr Solomon Philbrick I am, really, just like you or him,' with a jerk of the thumb towards the playing-fields, from which Mr Prendergast's voice could be heard crying weakly: 'Oh, do get into line, you beastly boys,' 'but *Sir* Solomon's what they call me. Out of respect, see?'

'When I say, "Are you ready? Go!" I want you to go,' Mr Prendergast could be heard saying. 'Are you ready? Go! Oh, why *don't* you go?' And his voice became drowned in shrill cries of protest.

'Mind you,' went on Philbrick, 'I haven't always been in the position that I am now. I was brought up rough, damned rough. Ever heard speak of "Chick" Philbrick?'

'No, I'm afraid not.'

'No, I suppose he was before your time. Useful little boxer, though. Not first-class, on account of his drinking so much *and* being short in the arm. Still, he used to earn five pound a night at the Lambeth Stadium. Always popular with the boys, he was, even when he was so full, he couldn't hardly fight. He was my dad, a good-hearted sort of fellow but rough, as I was telling you; he used to knock my poor mother about something awful. Got jugged for it twice, but my! he took it out of her when he got out. There aren't many left like him nowadays, what with education and whisky the price it is.'

' "Chick" was all for getting me on in the sporting world, and before I left school I was earning a few shillings a week holding the sponge at the Stadium on Saturday nights. It was there I met Toby Cruttwell. Perhaps you ain't heard of him, neither?'

'No, I am terribly afraid I haven't. I'm not very well up in sporting characters.'

'Sporting! What, Toby Cruttwell a sporting character! You make me laugh. Toby Cruttwell,' said Philbrick with renewed emphasis, 'what brought off the Buller diamond robbery of 1912, and the Amalgamated Steel Trust robbery of 1910, and the Isle of Wight burglaries in 1914? He wasn't no sporting character, Toby wasn't. Sporting character! D'you know what he done to Alf Larrigan, what tried to put it over on one of his girls? I'll tell you. Toby had a doctor in tow at the time, name of Peterfield; lives in Harley Street, with a swell lot of patients. Well, Toby knew a thing about him. He'd done in one of Toby's girls what went to him because she was going to have a kid. Well, Toby knew that, so he had to do what Toby told him, see?

'Toby didn't kill Alf; that wasn't his way. Toby never killed no one except a lot of blinking Turks the time they gave him the V.C. But he got hold of him and took him to Dr Peterfield, and – ' Philbrick's voice sank to a whisper.

'Second heat, get ready. Now, if you don't go when I say "Go", I shall disqualify you all; d'you hear? Are you ready? *Go!*'

' . . . He hadn't no use for girls after that. Ha, ha, ha! Sporting character's good. Well, me and Toby worked together for five years. I was with him in the Steel Trust and the Buller diamonds, and we cleared a nice little profit. Toby took 75 per cent, him being the older man, but even with that I did pretty well. Just before the war we split. He stuck to safe-cracking, and I settled down comfortable at the "Lamb and Flag", Camberwell Green. A very fine house that was before the war, and it's the best in the locality now, though I says it. Things aren't quite so easy as they was, but I can't complain. I've got the Picture House next to it, too. Just mention my name there any day you like to have a free seat.'

'That's very kind of you.'

'You're welcome. Well, then there was the war. Toby got the V.C. in the Dardanelles and turned respectable. He's in Parliament now – Major Cruttwell, M.P., Conservative member for some potty town on the South Coast. My old woman ran the pub for me. Didn't tell you I was married, did I? Pretty enough bit of goods when we was spliced, but she ran to fat. Women do in the public-house business. After the war things were a bit slow, and then my old woman kicked the bucket. I didn't think I'd mind much, her having got so fat and all, nor I didn't not at first, but after a time, when the excitement of the funeral had died down and things were going on just the same as usual, I began to get restless. You know how things get, and I took to reading the papers. Before that my old woman used to read out the bits she'd like, and sometimes I'd listen and sometimes I wouldn't, but anyhow they weren't the things that interested me. She never took no interest in crime, not unless it was a murder. But I took to reading the police news, and I took to dropping in at the pictures whenever they sent me a crook film. I didn't sleep so well, neither, and I used to lie awake thinking of old times. Of course I could have married again: in my position I could have married pretty well who I liked; but it wasn't that I wanted.

'Then one Saturday night I came into the bar. I generally drop in on Saturday evenings and smoke a cigar and stand a round of drinks. It sets the right tone. I wear a buttonhole in the summer, too, and a diamond ring. Well, I was in the saloon when who did I see in the corner but Jimmy Drage – cove I used to know when I was working with Toby Cruttwell. I never see a man look more discouraged.

' "Hullo, Jimmy!" I says. "We don't see each other as often as we used. How are things with you?" I says it cordial, but careful like, because I didn't know what Jimmy was up to.

' "Pretty bad," said Jimmy. "Just fooled a job."

' "What sort of job?" I says. "Nobbling," he says, meaning kidnapping.

' "It was like this," he says. 'You know a toff called Lord Utteridge?"

' "The bloke what had them electric burglar alarms," I says, "Utteridge House, Belgrave Square?"

' "That's the blinking bastard. Well, he's got a son – nasty little kid about twelve, just going off to college for the first time. I'd had my eye on him," Jimmy said, "for a long time, him being the only son and his father so rich, so when I'd finished the last job I was on I had a go at him. Everything went as easy as drinking," Jimmy said. There was a garage just round the corner behind Belgrave Square where he used to go every morning to watch them messing about with cars. Crazy about cars the kid was. Jimmy comes in one day with his motor-bike and side-car and asks for some petrol. He comes up and looks at it in the way he had.

' "That bike's no good," he says. "No good?" says Jimmy. "I wouldn't sell it not for a hundred quid, I wouldn't. This bike," he says, "won the Grand Prix at Boulogne." "Nonsense!" the kid says; "it wouldn't do thirty, not downhill." "Well, just you see," Jimmy says. "Come for a run? I bet you I'll do eighty on the road." In he got, and away they went till they got to a place Jimmy knew. Then Jimmy shuts him up safe and writes to the father. The kid was happy as blazes taking down the engine of Jimmy's bike. It's never been the same since, Jimmy told me, but then it wasn't much to talk of before. Everything had gone through splendid till Jimmy got his answer from Lord Utteridge. Would you believe it, that unnatural father wouldn't stump up, him that owns ships and coal mines enough to buy the blinking Bank of England. Said he was much obliged to Jimmy for the trouble he had taken, that the dearest wish of his life had been gratified and the one barrier to his complete happiness removed, but that, as the matter had been taken up without his instructions, he did not feel called upon to make any payment in respect of it, and remained his sincerely, Utteridge.

'That was a nasty one for Jimmy. He wrote once or twice after that, but got no answer, so by the time the kid had spread bits of the bike all over the room Jimmy let him go.

' "Did you try pulling out 'is teeth and sending them to his pa?" I asks.

' "No," says Jimmy, "I didn't do that."

'"Did you make the kid write pathetic, asking to be let out?"

'"No," says Jimmy, "I didn't do that."

' "Did you cut off one of his fingers and put it in the letter-box?"

' "No," he says.

' "Well, man alive," I says, "you don't deserve to succeed, you just don't know your job."

' "Oh, cut that out," he says; "it's easy to talk. You've been out of the business ten years. You don't know what things are like nowadays."

'Well, that rather set me thinking. As I say, I'd been getting restless doing nothing but just pottering round the pub all day. "Look here," I says, "I bet you I can bring off a job like that any day with any kid you like to mention." "Done!" says Jimmy. So he opens a newspaper. "The first toff we find what's got a' only son," he says. "Right!" says I. Well, about the first thing we found was a picture of Lady Circumference with her only son, Lord Tangent, at Warwick Races. "There's your man," says Jimmy. And that's what brought me here.'

'But, good gracious,' said Paul, 'why have you told me this monstrous story? I shall certainly inform the police. I never heard of such a thing.'

'That's all right,' said Philbrick. 'The job's off. Jimmy's won his bet. All this was before I met Dina, see?'

'Dina?'

'Miss Diana. Dina I calls her, after a song I heard. The moment I saw that girl I knew the game was up. My heart just stood still. There's a song about that, too. That girl,' said Philbrick, 'could bring a man up from the depths of hell itself.'

'You feel as strongly as that about her?'

'I'd go through fire and water for that girl. She's not happy here. I don't think her dad treats her proper. Sometimes,' said Philbrick, 'I think she's only marrying me to get away from here.'

'Good Heavens! Are you going to get married?'

'We fixed it up last Thursday. We've been going together for some time. It's bad for a girl being shut away like that, never seeing a man. She was in a state she'd have gone with anybody until I come along, just housekeeping day in, day out. The only pleasure she ever got was cutting down the bills and dismissing the servants. Most of them leave before their month is up, anyway, they're that hungry. She's got a head on her shoulders, she has. Real business woman, just what I need at the "Lamb".

'Then she heard me on the phone one day giving instructions to our manager at the Picture Theatre. That made her think a bit. A prince in disguise, as you might say. It was she who actually suggested our getting married. I shouldn't have had the face to, not while I was butler. What I'd meant to do was to hire a car one day and come down with my diamond ring and buttonhole and pop the question. But there wasn't any need for that. Love's a wonderful thing.'

Philbrick stopped speaking and was evidently deeply moved by his recital. The door of the pavilion opened, and Mr Prendergast came in.

'Well,' asked Paul, 'how are the sports going?'

'Not very well,' said Mr Prendergast; 'in fact, they've gone.'

'All over?'

'Yes. You see, none of the boys came back from the first race. They just disappeared behind the trees at the top of the drive. I expect they've gone to change. I don't blame them, I'm sure. It's terribly cold. Still, it was discouraging launching heat after heat and none coming back. Like sending troops into battle, you know.'

'The best thing for us to do is to go back and change too.'

'Yes, I suppose so. Oh, what a day!'

Grimes was in the Common Room.

'Just back from the gay metropolis of Llandudno,' he said. 'Shopping with Dingy is not a seemly occupation for a public school man. How did the heats go?'

'There weren't any,' said Paul.

'Quite right,' said Grimes: 'you leave this to me. I've been in the trade some time. These things are best done over the fire. We can make out the results in peace. We'd better hurry. The old boy wants them sent to be printed this evening.'

And taking a sheet of paper and a small stub of pencil, Grimes made out the programme.

'How about that?' he said.

'Clutterbuck seems to have done pretty well,' said Paul.

'Yes, he's a splendid little athlete,' said Grimes. 'Now just you telephone that through to the printers, and they'll get it done to-night. I wonder if we ought to have a hurdle race?'

'No,' said Mr Prendergast.

CHAPTER VIII
The Sports

HAPPILY enough, it did not rain next day, and after morning school everybody dressed up to the nines. Dr Fagan appeared in a pale grey morning coat and spongebag trousers, looking more than ever *jeune premier*; there was a spring in his step and a pronounced sprightliness of bearing that Paul had not observed before. Flossie wore a violet frock of knitted wool made for her during the preceding autumn by her sister. It was the colour of indelible ink on blotting paper, and was ornamented at the waist with flowers of emerald green and pink. Her hat, also home-made, was the outcome of many winter evenings of ungrudged labour. All the trimmings of all her previous hats had gone to its adornment. Dingy wore a little steel brooch made in the shape of a bull-dog. Grimes wore a stiff evening collar of celluloid.

'Had to do something to celebrate the occasion,' he said, 'so I put on a "choker". Phew, though, it's tight. Have you seen my fiancée's latest creation? Ascot ain't in it. Let's get down to Mrs Roberts for a quick one before the happy throng rolls up.'

'I wish I could, but I've got to go round the ground with the Doctor.'

'Righto, old boy! See you later. Here comes Prendy in his coat of many colours.'

Mr Prendergast wore a blazer of faded stripes, which smelt strongly of camphor.

'I think Dr Fagan encourages a certain amount of display on these occasions,' he said. 'I used to keep wicket for my college, you know, but I was too short-sighted to be much good. Still, I am entitled to the blazer,' he said with a note of defiance in his voice, 'and it is more appropriate to a sporting occasion than a stiff collar.'

'Good old Prendy!' said Grimes. 'Nothing like a change of clothes to bring out latent pep. I felt like that my first week in khaki. Well, so long. Me for Mrs Roberts. Why don't you come too, Prendy?'

'D'you know,' said Mr Prendergast, 'I think I will.'

Paul watched them disappear down the drive in amazement. Then he went off to find the Doctor.

'Frankly,' said the Doctor, 'I am at a loss to understand my own emotions. I can think of no entertainment that fills me with greater detestation than a display of competitive athletics, none – except possibly folk-dancing. If there are two women in the world whose company I abominate – and there are very many more than two – they are Mrs Beste-Chetwynde and Lady Circumference. I have, moreover, had an extremely difficult encounter with my butler, who – will you believe it? – waited at luncheon in a mustard-coloured suit of plus-fours and a diamond tie-pin, and when I reprimanded him, attempted to tell me some ridiculous story about his being the proprietor of a circus or swimming-bath or some such concern. And yet,' said the Doctor, 'I am filled with a wholly delightful exhilaration. I can't understand it. It is not as though this was the first occasion of the kind. During the fourteen years that I have been at Llanabba there have been six sports days and two concerts, all of them, in one way or another, utterly disastrous. Once Lady Bunyan was taken ill; another time it was the matter of the press photographers and the obstacle race; another time some quite unimportant parents brought a dog with them which bit two of the boys very severely and one of the masters, who swore terribly in front of everyone. I could hardly blame him, but of course he had to go. Then there was the concert when the boys refused to sing "God Save the King" because of the pudding they had had for luncheon. One way and another, I have been consistently unfortunate in my efforts at festivity. And yet I look forward to each new fiasco with the utmost relish. Perhaps, Pennyfeather, you will bring luck to Llanabba; in fact, I feel confident you have already done so. Look at the sun!'

Picking their way carefully among the dry patches in the waterlogged drive, they reached the playing-fields. Here the haphazard organization of the last twenty-four hours seemed to have been fairly successful. A large marquee was already in position, and Philbrick – still in plus-fours – and three gardeners were at work putting up a smaller tent.

'That's for the Llanabba Silver Band,' said the Doctor. 'Philbrick, I required you to take off those loathsome garments.'

'They were new when I bought them,' said Philbrick, 'and they cost eight pounds fifteen. Anyhow, I can't do two things at once, can I? If I go back to change, who's going to manage all this, I'd like to know?'

'All right! Finish what you are doing first. Let us just review the arrangements. The marquee is for the visitors' tea. That is Diana's province. I expect we shall find her at work.'

Sure enough, there was Dingy helping two servants to arrange plates of highly-coloured cakes down a trestle table. Two other servants in the background were cutting sandwiches. Dingy, too, was obviously enjoying herself.

'Jane, Emily, remember that that butter has to do for three loaves. Spread it thoroughly, but don't waste it, and cut the crusts as thin as possible. Father, will you see to it that the boys who come in with their parents come in *alone?* You remember last time how Briggs brought in four boys with him, and they ate all the jam sandwiches before Colonel Loder had

had any. Mr Pennyfeather, the champagne-cup is *not* for the masters. In fact, I expect you will find yourselves too much occupied helping the visitors to have any tea until they have left the tent. You had better tell Captain Grimes that, too. I am sure Mr Prendergast would not think of pushing himself forward.'

Outside the marquee were assembled several seats and tubs of palms and flowering shrubs. 'All this must be set in order,' said the Doctor; 'our guests may arrive in less than an hour.' He passed on. 'The cars shall turn aside from the drive here and come right into the ground. It will give a pleasant background to the photographs, and, Pennyfeather, if you would with tact direct the photographer so that more prominence was given to Mrs Beste-Chetwynde's Hispano Suiza than to Lady Circumference's little motor car, I think it would be all to the good. All these things count, you know.'

'Nothing seems to have been done about marking out the ground,' said Paul.

'No,' said the Doctor, turning his attention to the field for the first time, 'nothing. Well, you must do the best you can. They can't do everything.'

'I wonder if any hurdles have come?'

'They were ordered,' said the Doctor. 'I am certain of it. Philbrick, have any hurdles come?'

'Yes,' said Philbrick with a low chuckle.

'Why, pray, do you laugh at the mention of hurdles?'

'Just you look at them!' said Philbrick. 'They're behind the tea-house there.'

Paul and the Doctor went to look and found a pile of spiked iron railings in sections heaped up at the back of the marquee. They were each about five feet high and were painted green with gilt spikes.

'It seems to me that they have sent the wrong sort,' said the Doctor.

'Yes.'

'Well, we must do the best we can. What other things ought there to be?'

'Weight, hammer, javelin, long-jump pit, high-jump posts, low hurdles, eggs, spoons, and greasy pole,' said Philbrick.

'Previously competed for,' said the Doctor imperturbably. 'What else?'

'Somewhere to run,' suggested Paul.

'Why, God bless my soul, they've got the whole park! How did you manage yesterday for the heats?'

'We judged the distance by eye.'

'Then that is what we shall have to do to-day. Really, my dear Pennyfeather, it is quite unlike you to fabricate difficulties in this way. I am afraid you are getting unnerved. Let them go on racing until it is time for tea; and remember,' he added sagely, 'the longer the race the more time it takes. I leave the details to you. I am concerned with *style*. I wish, for instance, we had a starting pistol.'

'Would this be any use?' said Philbrick, producing an enormous service revolver. 'Only take care; it's loaded.'

'The very thing,' said the Doctor. 'Only fire into the ground, mind. We must do everything we can to avoid an accident. Do you always carry that about with you?'

'Only when I'm wearing my diamonds,' said Philbrick.

'Well, I hope that is not often. Good gracious! Who are these extraordinary-looking people?'

Ten men of revolting appearance were approaching from the drive. They were low of brow, crafty of eye, and crooked of limb. They advanced huddled together with the loping tread of wolves, peering about them furtively as they came, as though in constant terror of ambush; they slavered at their mouths, which hung loosely over their receding chins, while each clutched under his ape-like arm a burden of curious and unaccountable shape. On seeing the Doctor they halted and edged back, those behind squinting and moulting over their companions' shoulders.

'Crikey!' said Philbrick. 'Loonies! This is where I shoot.'

'I refuse to believe the evidence of my eyes,' said the Doctor. 'These creatures simply do not exist.'

After brief preliminary shuffling and nudging, an elderly man emerged from the back of the group. He had a rough black beard and wore on his uneven shoulders a druidical wreath of brass mistletoe-berries.

'Why, it's my friend the stationmaster!' said Philbrick.

'We are the silver band the Lord bless and keep you,' said the stationmaster in one breath, 'the band that no one could beat whatever but two indeed in the Eisteddfod that for all North Wales was look you.'

'I see,' said the Doctor; 'I see. That's splendid. Well, will you please go into your tent, the little tent over there.'

'To march about you would not like us?' suggested the stationmaster; 'we have a fine yellow flag look you that embroidered for us was in silks.'

'No, no. Into the tent!'

The stationmaster went back to consult with his fellow-musicians. There was a baying and growling and yapping as of the jungle at moonrise, and presently he came forward again with an obsequious, sidelong shuffle.

'Three pounds you pay us would you said indeed to at the sports play.'

'Yes, yes, that's right, three pounds. Into the tent!'

'Nothing whatever we can play without the money first,' said the stationmaster firmly.

'How would it be,' said Philbrick, 'if I gave him a clout on the ear?'

'No, no, I beg you to do nothing of the kind. You have not lived in Wales as long as I have.' He took a note-case from his pocket, the sight of which seemed to galvanize the musicians into life; they crowded round, twitching and chattering. The Doctor took out three pound notes and gave them to the stationmaster. 'There you are, Davies!' he said. 'Now take your men into the tent. They are on no account to emerge until after tea; do you understand?'

The band slunk away, and Paul and the Doctor turned back towards the Castle.

'The Welsh character is an interesting study,' said Dr Fagan. 'I have often considered writing a little monograph on the subject, but I was afraid it might make me unpopular in the village. The ignorant speak of them as Celts, which is of course wholly erroneous. They are of pure Iberian stock – the aboriginal inhabitants of Europe who survive only in Portugal and the Basque district. Celts readily intermarry with their neighbours and absorb them. From the earliest times the Welsh have been looked upon as an unclean people. It is thus that they have preserved their racial integrity. Their sons and daughters rarely mate with human-kind except their own blood relations. In Wales there was no need for legislation to prevent the conquering people intermarrying with the conquered. In Ireland that was necessary, for there intermarriage was a political matter. In Wales it was moral. I hope, by the way, you have no Welsh blood?'

'None whatever,' said Paul.

'I was sure you had not, but one cannot be too careful. I once spoke of this subject to the sixth form and learned later that one of them had a Welsh grandmother. I am afraid it hurt his feelings terribly, poor little chap. She came from Pembrokeshire, too, which is of course quite a different matter. I often think,' he continued, 'that we can trace almost all the disasters of English history to the influence of Wales. Think of Edward of Caernarvon, the first Prince of Wales, a perverse life, Pennyfeather, and an unseemly death, then the Tudors and the dissolution of the Church, then Lloyd George, the temperance movement, Nonconformity, and lust stalking hand in hand through the country, wasting and ravaging. But perhaps you think I exaggerate? I have a certain rhetorical tendency, I admit.'

'No, no,' said Paul.

'The Welsh,' said the Doctor, 'are the only nation in the world that has produced no graphic or plastic art, no architecture, no drama. They just sing,' he said with disgust, 'sing and blow down wind instruments of plated silver. They are deceitful because they cannot discern truth from falsehood, depraved because they cannot discern the consequences of their indulgence. Let us consider,' he continued, 'the etymological derivations of the Welsh language. . . .'

But here he was interrupted by a breathless little boy who panted down the drive to meet them. 'Please, sir, Lord and Lady Circumference have arrived sir. They're in the library with Miss Florence. She asked me to tell you.'

'The sports will start in ten minutes,' said the Doctor. 'Run and tell the other boys to change and go at once to the playing-fields. I will talk to you about the Welsh again. It is a matter to which I have given some thought, and I can see that you are sincerely interested. Come in with me and see the Circumferences.'

Flossie was talking to them in the library.

'Yes, isn't it a sweet colour?' she was saying. 'I do like something bright myself. Diana made it for me; she does knit a treat, does Diana, but of course I chose the colour, you know, because, you see, Diana's taste is all for wishy-washy greys and browns. Mournful, you know. Well, here's the dad. Lady Circumference was just saying how much she likes my frock what you said was vulgar, so there!'

A stout elderly woman dressed in a tweed coat and skirt and jaunty Tyrolean hat advanced to the Doctor. 'Hullo!' she said in a deep bass voice, 'how are you? Sorry if we're late. Circumference ran over a fool of a boy. I've just been chaffing your daughter here about her frock. Wish I was young enough to wear that kind of thing. Older I get the more I like colour. We're both pretty long in the tooth, eh?' She gave Dr Fagan a hearty shake of the hand, that obviously caused him acute pain. Then she turned to Paul.

'So you're the Doctor's hired assassin, eh? Well, I hope you keep a firm hand on my toad of a son. How's he doin'?'

'Quite well,' said Paul.

'Nonsense!' said Lady Circumference. 'The boy's a dunderhead. If he wasn't he wouldn't be here. He wants beatin' and hittin' and knockin' about generally, and then he'll be no good. That grass is shockin' bad on the terrace, Doctor; you ought to sand it down and re-sow it, but you'll have to take that cedar down if you ever want it to grow properly at the side. I hate cuttin' down a tree – like losin' a tooth – but you have to choose, tree or grass; you can't keep 'em both. What d'you pay your head man?'

As she was talking Lord Circumference emerged from the shadows and shook Paul's hand. He had a long fair moustache and large watery eyes which reminded Paul a little of Mr Prendergast.

'How do you do?' he said.

'How do you do?' said Paul.

'Fond of sport, eh?' he said. 'I mean these sort of sports?'

'Oh, yes,' said Paul. 'I think they're so good for the boys.'

'Do you? Do you think that,' said Lord Circumference very earnestly: 'you think they're good for the boys?'

'Yes,' said Paul; 'don't you?'

'Me? Yes, oh yes. I think so, too. Very good for the boys.'

'So useful in the case of a war or anything,' said Paul.

'Do you think so? D'you really and truly think so? That there's going to be another war, I mean?'

'Yes, I'm sure of it; aren't you?'

'Yes, of course. I'm sure of it too. And that awful bread, and people coming on to one's own land and telling one what one's to do with one's own butter and milk, and commandeering one's horses! Oh, yes all over again! My wife shot her hunters rather than let them go to the army. And girls in breeches on all the farms! All over again! Who do you think it will be this time?'

'The Americans,' said Paul stoutly.

'No, indeed, I hope not. We had German prisoners on two of the farms. That wasn't so bad, but if they start putting Americans on my land, I'll just refuse to stand it. My daughter brought an American down to luncheon the other day, and, do you know . . . ?'

'Dig it and dung it,' said Lady Circumference. 'Only it's got to be dug deep, mind. Now how did your calceolarias do last year?'

'I really have no idea,' said the Doctor. 'Flossie, how did our calceolarias do?'

'Lovely,' said Flossie.

'I don't believe a word of it,' said Lady Circumference. 'Nobody's calceolarias did well last year.'

'Shall we adjourn to the playing-fields?' said the Doctor. 'I expect they are all waiting for us.'

Talking cheerfully, the party crossed the hall and went down the steps.

'Your drive's awful wet,' said Lady Circumference. 'I expect there's a blocked pipe somewhere. Sure it ain't sewage?'

'I was never any use at short distances,' Lord Circumference was saying. 'I was always a slow starter, but I was once eighteenth in the Crick at Rugby. We didn't take sports so seriously at the 'Varsity when I was up: everybody rode. What college were you at?'

'Scone.'

'Scone, were you? Ever come across a young nephew of my wife's called Alastair Digby-Vane-Trumpington?'

'I just met him,' said Paul.

'That's very interesting, Greta. Mr Pennyfoot knows Alastair.'

'Does he? Well, that boy's doing no good for himself. Got fined twenty pounds the other day, his mother told me. Seemed proud of it. If my brother had been alive he'd have licked all that out of the young cub. It takes a man to bring up a man.'

'Yes,' said Lord Circumference meekly.

'Who else do you know at Oxford? Do you know Freddy French-Wise?'

'No.'

'Or Tom Obblethwaite or that youngest Castleton boy?'

'No, I'm afraid not. I had a great friend called Potts.'

'*Potts!*' said Lady Circumference, and left it at that.

All the school and several local visitors were assembled in the field. Grimes stood by himself, looking depressed. Mr Prendergast, flushed and unusually vivacious, was talking to the Vicar. As the headmaster's party came into sight the Llanabba Silver Band struck up *Men of Harlech*.

'Shockin' noise,' commented Lady Circumference graciously.

The head prefect came forward and presented her with a programme, be-ribboned and embossed in gold. Another prefect set a chair for her. She sat down with the Doctor next to her and Lord Circumference on the other side of him.

'Pennyfeather,' cried the Doctor above the band, 'start them racing.'

Philbrick gave Paul a megaphone. 'I found this in the pavilion,' he said. 'I thought it might be useful.'

'Who's that extraordinary man?' asked Lady Circumference.

'He is the boxing coach and swimming professional,' said the Doctor. 'A finely developed figure, don't you think?'

'First race,' said Paul through the megaphone, 'under sixteen. Quarter-mile!' He read out Grimes' list of starters.

'What's Tangent doin' in this race?' said Lady Circumference. 'The boy can't run an inch.'

The silver band stopped playing.

'The course,' said Paul, 'starts from the pavilion, goes round that clump of elms . . .'

'Beeches,' corrected Lady Circumference loudly.

'. . . and ends in front of the bandstand. Starter, Mr Prendergast; timekeeper, Captain Grimes.'

'I shall say, "Are you ready? one, two, three!" and then fire,' said Mr Prendergast. 'Are you ready? One' – there was a terrific report. 'Oh dear! I'm sorry' – but the race had begun. Clearly Tangent was not going to win; he was sitting on the grass crying because he had been wounded in the foot by Mr Prendergast's bullet. Philbrick carried him, wailing dismally, into the refreshment tent, where Dingy helped him off with his shoe. His heel was slightly grazed. Dingy gave him a large slice of cake, and he hobbled out surrounded by a sympathetic crowd.

'That won't hurt him,' said Lady Circumference, 'but I think someone ought to remove the pistol from that old man before he does anything serious.'

'I knew that was going to happen,' said Lord Circumference.

'A most unfortunate beginning,' said the Doctor.

'Am I going to die?' said Tangent, his mouth full of cake.

'For God's sake, look after Prendy,' said Grimes in Paul's ear. 'The man's as tight as a lord, and on one whisky, too.'

'First blood to me!' said Mr Prendergast gleefully.

'The last race will be run again,' said Paul down the megaphone. 'Starter, Mr Philbrick; timekeeper, Mr Prendergast.'

'On your marks! Get set.' Bang went the pistol, this time without disaster. The six little boys scampered off through the mud, disappeared behind the beeches and returned rather more slowly. Captain Grimes and Mr Prendergast held up a piece of tape.

'Well run, sir!' shouted Colonel Sidebotham. 'Jolly good race.'

'Capital,' said Mr Prendergast, and dropping his end of the tape, he sauntered over to the Colonel. 'I can see you are a fine judge of a race, sir. So was I once. So's Grimes. A capital fellow, Grimes; a bounder, you know, but a capital fellow. Bounders can be capital fellows; don't you agree, Colonel Slidebottom? In fact, I'd go further and say that capital fellows *are* bounders. What d'you say to that? I wish you'd stop pulling at my arm, Pennyfeather. Colonel Shybottom and I are just having a most interesting conversation about bounders.'

The silver band struck up again, and Mr Prendergast began a little jig, saying: 'Capital fellow!' and snapping his fingers. Paul led him to the refreshment tent.

'Dingy wants you to help her in there,' he said firmly, 'and, for God's sake, don't come out until you feel better.'

'I never felt better in my life,' said Mr Prendergast indignantly. 'Capital fellow! capital fellow!'

'It is not my affair, of course,' said Colonel Sidebotham, 'but if you ask me I should say that man had been drinking.'

'He was talking very excitedly to me,' said the Vicar, 'about some apparatus for warming a church in Worthing and about the Apostolic Claims of the Church of Abyssinia. I confess I could not follow him clearly. He seems deeply interested in Church matters. Are you quite sure he is right in the head? I have noticed again and again since I have been in the Church that lay interest in ecclesiastical matters is often a prelude to insanity.'

'Drink, pure and simple,' said the Colonel. 'I wonder where he got it? I could do with a spot of whisky.'

'Quarter-mile open!' said Paul through his megaphone.

Presently the Clutterbucks arrived. Both the parents were stout. They brought with them two small children, a governess, and an elder son. They debouched from the car one by one, stretching their limbs in evident relief.

'This is Sam,' said Mr Clutterbuck, 'just down from Cambridge. He's joined me in the business, and we've brought the nippers along for a treat. Don't mind, do you, Doc? And last, but not least, my wife.'

Dr Fagan greeted them with genial condescension and found them seats.

'I am afraid you have missed all the jumping events,' he said. 'But I have a list of the results here. You will see that Percy has done extremely well.'

'Didn't know the little beggar had it in him. See that, Martha? Percy's won the high-jump and the long-jump and the hurdles. How's your young hopeful been doing, Lady Circumference?'

'My boy has been injured in the foot,' said Lady Circumference coldly.

'Dear me! Not badly, I hope? Did he twist his ankle in the jumping?'

'No,' said Lady Circumference, 'he was shot at by one of the assistant masters. But it is kind of you to inquire.'

'Three Miles Open!' announced Paul. 'The course of six laps will be run as before.'

'On your marks! Get set.' Bang went Philbrick's revolver. Off trotted the boys on another race.

'Father,' said Flossie, 'don't you think it's time for the tea interval?'

'Nothing can be done before Mrs Beste-Chetwynde arrives,' said the Doctor.

Round and round the muddy track trotted the athletes while the silver band played sacred music unceasingly.

'Last lap!' announced Paul.

The school and the visitors crowded about the tape to cheer the winner. Amid loud applause Clutterbuck breasted the tape well ahead of the others.

'Well run! Oh, good, jolly good, sir!' cried Colonel Sidebotham.

'Good old Percy! That's the stuff,' said Mr Clutterbuck.

'Well run, Percy!' chorused the two little Clutterbucks, prompted by their governess.

'That boy cheated,' said Lady Circumference. 'He only went round five times. I counted.'

'I think unpleasantness so mars the afternoon,' said the Vicar.

'How dare you suggest such a thing?' asked Mrs Clutterbuck. 'I appeal to the referee. Percy ran the full course, didn't he?'

'Clutterbuck wins,' said Captain Grimes.

'Fiddlesticks!' said Lady Circumference. 'He deliberately lagged behind and joined the others as they went behind the beeches. The little toad!'

'Really, Greta,' said Lord Circumference, 'I think we ought to abide by the referee's decision.'

'Well, they can't expect me to give away the prizes, then. Nothing would induce me to give that boy a prize.'

'Do you understand, madam, that you are bringing a serious accusation against my son's honour?'

'Serious accusation fiddlesticks! What he wants is a jolly good hidin'.'

'No doubt you judge other people's sons by your own. Let me tell you, Lady Circumference . . .'

'Don't attempt to browbeat me, sir. I know a cheat when I see one.'

At this stage of the discussion the Doctor left Mrs Hope-Browne's side, where he had been remarking upon her son's progress in geometry, and joined the group round the winning-post.

'If there is a disputed decision,' he said genially, 'they shall race again.'

'Percy has won already,' said Mr Clutterbuck. 'He has been adjudged the winner.'

'Splendid! splendid! A promising little athlete. I congratulate you, Clutterbuck.'

'But he only ran five laps,' said Lady Circumference.

'Then clearly he has won the five furlongs race, a very exacting length.'

'But the other boys,' said Lady Circumference, almost beside herself with rage, 'have run six lengths.'

'Then they,' said the Doctor imperturbably, 'are first, second, third, fourth, and fifth respectively in the Three Miles. Clearly there has been some confusion. Diana, I think we might now serve tea.'

Things were not easy, but there was fortunately a distraction, for as he spoke an enormous limousine of dove-grey and silver stole soundlessly on to the field.

'But what could be more opportune? Here is Mrs Beste-Chetwynde.'

Three light skips brought him to the side of the car, but the footman was there before him. The door opened, and from the cushions within emerged a tall young man in a clinging dove-grey overcoat. After him, like the first breath of spring in the Champs-Élysées, came Mrs Beste-Chetwynde – two lizard-skin feet, silk legs, chinchilla body, a tight little black hat, pinned with platinum and diamonds, and the high invariable voice that may be heard in any Ritz Hotel from New York to Budapest.

'I hope you don't mind my bringing Chokey, Dr Fagan?' she said. 'He's just crazy about sport.'

'I sure am that,' said Chokey.

'Dear Mrs Beste-Chetwynde!' said Dr Fagan; 'dear, dear, Mrs Beste-Chetwynde!' He pressed her glove, and for the moment was at a loss for words of welcome, for 'Chokey', though graceful of bearing and irreproachably dressed, was a Negro.

CHAPTER IX
The Sports — continued

THE refreshment tent looked very nice. The long table across the centre was covered with a white cloth. Bowls of flowers were ranged down it at regular intervals, and between them plates of sandwiches and cakes and jugs of lemonade and champagne-cup. Behind it against a background of palms stood the four Welsh housemaids in clean caps and aprons pouring out tea. Behind them again sat Mr Prendergast, a glass of champagne-cup in his hand, his wig slightly awry. He rose unsteadily to his feet at the approach of the guests, made a little bow, and then sat down again rather suddenly.

'Will you take round the *foie gras* sandwiches, Mr Penny-feather?' said Dingy. 'They are not for the boys or Captain Grimes.'

'One for little me!' said Flossie as he passed her.

Philbrick, evidently regarding himself as one of the guests, was engaged in a heated discussion on greyhound-racing with Sam Clutterbuck.

'What price the coon?' he asked as Paul gave him a sandwich.

'It does my heart good to see old Prendy enjoying himself,' said Grimes. 'Pity he shot that kid, though.'

'There's not much the matter with him to see the way he's eating his tea. I say, this is rather a poor afternoon, isn't it?'

'Circulate, old boy, circulate. Things aren't going too smoothly.'

Nor indeed were they. The sudden ebullition of ill-feeling over the Three-Mile race, though checked by the arrival of Mrs Beste-Chetwynde, was by no means forgotten. There were two distinctly hostile camps in the tea-tent. On one side stood the Circumferences, Tangent, the Vicar, Colonel Sidebotham, and the Hope-Brownes; on the other the seven Clutterbucks, Philbrick, Flossie, and two or three parents who had been snubbed already that afternoon by Lady Circumference. No one spoke of the race, but outraged sportsmanship glinted perilously in every eye. Several parents, intent on their tea, crowded round Dingy and the table. Eminently aloof from all these stood Chokey and Mrs Beste-Chetwynde. Clearly the social balance was delicately poised, and the issue depended upon them. With or without her nigger, Mrs Beste-Chetwynde was a woman of vital importance.

'Why, Dr Fagan,' she was saying, 'it is too disappointing that we've missed the sports. We had just the slowest journey, stopping all the time to see the churches. You can't move Chokey once he's seen an old church. He's just crazy about culture, aren't you, darling?'

'I sure am that,' said Chokey.

'Are you interested in music?' said the Doctor tactfully.

'Well, just you hear that, Baby,' said Chokey; 'am *I* interested in music? I should say I am.'

'He plays just too divinely,' said Mrs Beste-Chetwynde.

'Has he heard my new records, would you say?'

'No, darling, I don't expect he has.'

'Well, just you hear *them*, sir, and then you'll know – am I interested in music.'

'Now, darling, don't get discouraged. I'll take you over and introduce you to Lady Circumference. It's his inferiority complex, the angel. He's just crazy to meet the aristocracy, aren't you, my sweet?'

'I sure am that,' said Chokey.

'I think it's an insult bringing a nigger here,' said Mrs Clutterbuck. 'It's an insult to our own women.'

'Niggers are all right,' said Philbrick. 'Where I draw a line is a Chink, nasty inhuman things. I had a pal bumped off by a Chink once. Throat cut horrible, it was, from ear to ear.'

'Good gracious!' said the Clutterbuck governess; 'was that in the Boxer rising?'

'No,' said Philbrick cheerfully. 'Saturday night in the Edgware Road. Might have happened to any of us.'

'What did the gentleman say?' asked the children.

'Never you mind, my dears. Run and have some more of the green cake.'

They ran off obediently, but the little boy was later heard whispering to his sister as she knelt at her prayers, 'cut horrible from ear to ear', so that until quite late in her life Miss Clutterbuck would feel a little faint when she saw a bus that was going to the Edgware Road.

'I've got a friend lives in Savannah,' said Sam, 'and he's told me a thing or two about niggers. Of course it's hardly a thing to talk about before the ladies, but, to put it bluntly, *they have uncontrollable passions*. See what I mean?'

'What a terrible thing!' said Grimes.

'You can't blame 'em, mind; it's just their nature. Animal, you know. Still, what I do say is, since they're like that, the less we see of them the better.'

'Quite,' said Mr Clutterbuck.

'I had such a curious conversation just now,' Lord Circumference was saying to Paul, 'with your bandmaster over there. He asked me whether I should like to meet his sister-in-law; and when I said, "Yes, I should be delighted to," he said that it would cost a pound normally, but that he'd let me have special terms. What *can* he have meant, Mr Pennyfoot?'

''Pon my soul,' Colonel Sidebotham was saying to the Vicar, 'I don't like the look of that nigger. I saw enough of Fuzzy-Wuzzy in the Soudan – devilish good enemy and devilish bad friend. I'm going across to talk to Mrs Clutterbuck. Between ourselves, I think Lady C. went a bit far. I didn't see the race myself, but there are limits. . . .'

'Rain ain't doin' the turnip crop any good,' Lady Circumference was saying.

'No, indeed,' said Mrs Beste-Chetwynde. 'Are you in England for long?'

'Why, I live in England, of course,' said Lady Circumference.

'My dear, how divine! But don't you find it just too expensive?'

This was one of Lady Circumference's favourite topics, but somehow she did not feel disposed to enlarge on it to Mrs Beste-Chetwynde with the same gusto as when she was talking to Mrs Sidebotham and the Vicar's wife. She never felt quite at ease with people richer than herself.

'Well, we all feel the wind a bit since the war,' she said briefly. 'How's Bobby Pastmaster?'

'Dotty,' said Mrs Beste-Chetwynde, 'terribly dotty, and he and Chokey don't get on. You'll like Chokey. He's just crazy about England, too. We've been around all the cathedrals, and now we're going to start on the country houses. We were thinking of running over to see you at Castle Tangent one afternoon.'

'That would be delightful, but I'm afraid we are in London at present. Which did you like best of the cathedrals, Mr Chokey?'

'Chokey's not really his name, you know. The angel's called "Mr Sebastian Cholmondley." '

'Well,' said Mr Cholmondley, 'they were all fine, just fine. When I saw the cathedrals my heart just rose up and sang within me. I sure am crazy about culture. You folk think because we're coloured we don't care about nothing but jazz. Why, I'd give all the jazz in the world for just one little stone from one of your cathedrals.'

'It's quite true. He would.'

'Well, that's most interesting, Mr Cholmondley. I used to live just outside Salisbury when I was a girl, but, little as I like jazz, I never felt quite as strongly as that about it.'

'Salisbury is full of historical interest, Lady Circumference, but in my opinion York Minster is the more refined.'

'Oh, you angel!' said Mrs Beste-Chetwynde. 'I could eat you up every bit.'

'And is this your first visit to an English school?' asked the Doctor.

'I should say not. Will you tell the Doctor the schools I've seen?'

'He's been to them all, even the quite new ones. In fact, he liked the new ones best.'

'They were more spacious. Have you ever seen Oxford?'

'Yes; in fact, I was educated there.'

'Were you, now? I've seen Oxford and Cambridge and Eton and Harrow. That's me all over. That's what I like, see? *I* appreciate art. There's plenty coloured people come over here and don't see nothing but a few night clubs. I read Shakespeare,' said Chokey, '*Hamlet, Macbeth, King Lear*. Ever read them?'

'Yes,' said the Doctor; 'as a matter of fact, I have.'

'My race,' said Chokey, 'is essentially an artistic race. We have the child's love of song and colour and the child's natural good taste. All you white folks despise the poor coloured man. . . .'

'No, no,' said the Doctor.

'Let him say his piece, the darling,' said Mrs Beste-Chetwynde. 'Isn't he divine!'

'You folks all think the coloured man hasn't got a soul. Anything's good enough for the poor coloured man. Beat him; put him in chains; load him with burdens. . . .' Here Paul observed a responsive glitter in Lady Circumference's eye. 'But all the time that poor coloured man has a soul same as you have. Don't he breathe the same as you? Don't he eat and drink? Don't he love Shakespeare and cathedrals and the paintings of the old masters same as you? Isn't he just asking for your love and help to raise him from the servitude into which your forefathers plunged him? Oh, say, white folks, why don't you stretch out a helping hand to the poor coloured man, that's as good as you are, if you'll only let him be?'

'My sweet,' said Mrs Beste-Chetwynde, 'you mustn't get discouraged. They're all friends here.'

'Is that so?' said Chokey. 'Should I sing them a song?'

'No, don't do that, darling. Have some tea.'

'I had a friend in Paris,' said the Clutterbuck governess, 'whose sister knew a girl who married one of the black soldiers during the war, and you wouldn't believe what he did to her. Joan and Peter, run and see if Daddy wants some more tea. He tied her up with a razor strop and left her on the stone floor for the night without food or covering. And then it was over a year before she could get a divorce.'

'Used to cut off the tent ropes,' Colonel Sidebotham was saying, 'and then knife the poor beggars through the canvas.'

'You can see 'em in Shaftesbury Avenue and Charing Cross Road any night of the week,' Sam Clutterbuck was saying. 'The women just hanging on to 'em.'

'The mistake was ever giving them their freedom,' said the Vicar. 'They were far happier and better looked after before.'

'It's queer,' said Flossie, 'that a woman with as much money as Mrs Beste-Chetwynde should wear such *dull* clothes.'

'That ring didn't cost less than five hundred,' said Philbrick.

'Let's go and talk to the Vicar about God,' said Mrs Beste-Chetwynde. 'Chokey thinks religion is just divine.'

'My race is a very spiritual one,' said Chokey.

'The band has been playing *Men of Harlech* for over half an hour,' said the Doctor. 'Diana, do go and tell them to try something else.'

'I sometimes think I'm getting rather bored with coloured people,' Mrs Beste-Chetwynde said to Lady Circumference. 'Are you?'

'I have never had the opportunity.'

'I daresay you'd be good with them. They take a lot of living up to; they *are* so earnest. Who's that dear, dim, drunk little man?'

'That is the person who shot my son.'

'My dear, how too shattering for you. Not dead, I hope? Chokey shot a man at a party the other night. He gets gay at times, you know. It's only when he's on his best behaviour that he's so class-conscious. I must go and rescue the Vicar.'

The stationmaster came into the tent, crab-like and obsequious.

'Well, my good man?' said the Doctor.

'The young lady I have been telling that no other tunes can we play whatever with the lady smoking at her cigarette look you.'

'God bless my soul. Why not?'

'The other tunes are all holy tunes look you. Blasphemy it would be to play the songs of Sion while the lady at a cigarette smokes whatever. *Men of Harlech* is good music look you.'

'This is most unfortunate. I can hardly ask Mrs Beste-Chetwynde to stop smoking. Frankly I regard this as impertinence.'

'But no man can you ask against his Maker to blaspheme whatever unless him to pay more you were. Three pounds for the music is good and one for blasphemy look you.'

Dr Fagan gave him another pound. The stationmaster retired, and in a few minutes the silver band began a singularly emotional rendering of *In Thy courts no more are needed Sun by day and Moon by night.*

CHAPTER X
Post Mortem

AS the last car drove away the Doctor and his daughters and Paul and Grimes walked up the drive together towards the Castle.

'Frankly the day has been rather a disappointment to me,' said the Doctor. 'Nothing seemed to go quite right in spite of all our preparations.'

'And expense,' said Dingy.

'I am sorry, too, that Mr Prendergast should have had that unfortunate disagreement with Mrs Beste-Chetwynde's coloured friend. In all the ten years during which we have worked together I have never known Mr Prendergast so self-assertive. It was *not* becoming of him. Nor was it Philbrick's place to join in. I was seriously alarmed. They seemed so angry, and all about some minor point of ecclesiastical architecture.'

'Mr Cholmondley was very sensitive,' said Flossie.

'Yes, he seemed to think that Mr Prendergast's insistence on the late development of the rood-screen was in some way connected with colour-prejudice. I wonder why that was?

To my mind it showed a very confused line of thought. Still, it would have been more seemly if Mr Prendergast had let the matter drop, and what could Philbrick know of the matter?'

'Philbrick is not an ordinary butler,' said Dingy.

'No, indeed not,' said the Doctor. 'I heartily deplore his jewellery.'

'I didn't like Lady Circumference's speech,' said Flossie. 'Did you?'

'I did not,' said the Doctor; 'nor, I think, did Mrs Clutterbuck. I thought her reference to the Five Furlong race positively brutal. I was glad Clutterbuck had done so well in the jumping yesterday.'

'She rather wanders from the point, doesn't she?' said Dingy. 'All that about hunting, I mean.'

'I don't think Lady Circumference is conscious of any definite divisions in the various branches of sport. I have often observed in women of her type a tendency to regard all athletics as inferior forms of foxhunting. It is *not* logical. Besides, she was nettled at some remark of Mr Cholmondley's about cruelty to animals. As you say, it was irrelevant and rather unfortunate. I also resented the reference to the Liberal Party. Mr Clutterbuck has stood three times, you know. Taken as a whole, it was *not* a happy speech. I was quite glad when I saw her drive away.'

'What a pretty car Mrs Beste-Chetwynde has got!' said Flossie, 'but how ostentatious of her to bring a footman.'

'I can forgive the footman,' said Dingy, 'but I can't forgive Mr Cholmondley. He asked me whether I had ever heard of a writer called Thomas Hardy.'

'He asked *me* to go to Reigate with him for the weekend,' said Flossie, ' . . . in rather a sweet way, too.'

'Florence, I trust you refused?'

'Oh, yes,' said Flossie sadly, 'I refused.'

They went on up the drive in silence. Presently Dingy asked: 'What are we going to do about those fireworks you insisted on buying? Everyone has gone away.'

'I don't feel in a mood for fireworks,' said the Doctor. 'Perhaps another time, but not now.'

*

Back in the Common Room, Paul and Grimes subsided moodily into the two easy-chairs. The fire, unattended since luncheon, had sunk to a handful of warm ashes.

'Well, old boy,' said Grimes, 'so that's over.'

'Yes,' said Paul.

'All the gay throng melted away?'

'Yes,' said Paul.

'Back to the daily round and cloistral calm?'

'Yes,' said Paul.

'As a beano,' said Grimes, 'I have known better.'

'Yes,' said Paul.

'Lady C.'s hardly what you might call bonhommous.'

'Hardly.'

'Old Prendy made rather an ass of himself?'

'Yes.'

'Hullo, old boy! You sound a bit flat. Feeling the strain of the social vortex, a bit giddy after the gay whirl, eh?'

'I say, Grimes,' said Paul, 'what d'you suppose the relationship is between Mrs Beste-Chetwynde and that nigger?'

'Well, I don't suppose she trots with him just for the uplift of his conversation; do you?'

'No, I suppose not.'

'In fact, I don't mind diagnosing a simple case of good old sex.'

'Yes, I suppose you're right.'

'I'm sure of it. Great Scott, what's that noise?'

It was Mr Prendergast.

'Prendy, old man,' said Grimes, 'you've let down the morale of the Common Room a pretty good wallop.'

'Damn the Common Room!' said Mr Prendergast. 'What does the Common Room know about rood-screens?'

'That's all right, old boy. We're all friends here. What you say about rood-screens goes.'

'They'll be questioning the efficacy of infant baptism next. The Church has never countenanced lay opinion on spiritual matters. Now if it were a question of food and drink,' said Mr Prendergast, 'if it were a question of drink − But not infant baptism. Just drink.' And he sat down.

'A sad case, brother,' said Grimes, 'truly a sad case. Prendy, do you realize that in two minutes the bell will go for Prep. and you're on duty?'

'Ding, dong, dell! Pussy's in the well.'

'Prendy, that's irrelevant.'

'I know several songs about bells. Funeral bells, wedding-bells, sacring bells, sheep-bells, fire-bells, door-bells, dumb-bells, and just plain bells.'

Paul and Grimes looked at each other sadly.

'It seems to me,' said Paul, 'that one of us will have to take Prep. for him to-night.'

'No, no, old boy; that'll be all right,' said Grimes. 'You and I are off to Mrs Roberts. Prendy gives me a thirst.'

'But we can't leave him like this.'

'He'll be all right. The little beasts can't make any more noise than they do usually.'

'You don't think the old man will find him?'

'Not a chance.'

The bell rang. Mr Prendergast jumped to his feet, straightened his wig and steadied himself gravely against the chimney-piece.

'There's a good chap,' said Grimes gently. 'Just you trot down the passage to the little boys and have a good nap.'

Singing quietly to himself, Mr Prendergast sauntered down the passage.

'I hope he's none the worse for this,' said Grimes. 'You know, I feel quite fatherly towards old Prendy. He did give it to that blackamoor about Church architecture, bless him.'

Arm in arm they went down the main avenue towards the inn.

'Mrs Beste-Chetwynde asked me to call on her in London,' said Paul.

'Did she? Well, just you go. I've never been much of a one for society and the smart set myself, but if you like that sort of thing, Mrs Beste-Chetwynde is the goods all right. Never open a paper but there's a photograph of her at some place or other.'

'Does she photograph well?' asked Paul. 'I should rather think that she would.'

Grimes looked at him narrowly. 'Fair to middling. Why the sudden interest?'

'Oh, I don't know. I was just wondering.'

At Mrs Roberts' they found the Llanabba Silver Band chattering acrimoniously over the division of the spoils.

'All the afternoon the band I have led in *Men of Harlech* and sacred music too look you and they will not give me a penny more than themselves whatever. The college gentleman whatever if it is right I ask,' said the stationmaster, 'me with a sister-in-law to support too look you.'

'Now don't bother, old boy,' said Grimes, 'because, if you do, I'll tell your pals about the extra pound you got out of the Doctor.'

The discussion was resumed in Welsh, but it was clear that the stationmaster was slowly giving way.

'That's settled him all right. Take my tip, old boy; never get mixed up in a Welsh wrangle. It doesn't end in blows, like an Irish one, but goes on for ever. They'll still be discussing that three pounds at the end of term; just you see.'

'Has Mr Beste-Chetwynde been dead long?' asked Paul.

'I shouldn't say so; why?'

'I was just wondering.'

They sat for some time smoking in silence.

'If Beste-Chetwynde is fifteen,' said Paul, 'that doesn't necessarily make her more than thirty-one, does it?'

'Old boy,' said Grimes, 'you're in love.'

'Nonsense!'

'Smitten?' said Grimes.

'No, no.'

'The tender passion?'

'No.'

'Cupid's jolly little darts?'

'No.'

'Spring fancies, love's young dream?'

'Nonsense!'

'Not even a quickening of the pulse?'

'No.'

'A sweet despair?'

'Certainly not.'

'A trembling hope?'

'No.'

'A *frisson*? a *Je ne sais quoi*?'

'Nothing of the sort.'

'Liar!' said Grimes.

There was another long pause. 'Grimes,' said Paul at length, 'I wonder if you can be right?'

'Sure of it, old boy. Just you go in and win. Here's to the happy pair! May all your troubles be little ones.'

In a state of mind totally new to him, Paul accompanied Grimes back to the Castle. Prep. was over. Mr Prendergast was leaning against the fireplace with a contented smile on his face.

'Hullo, Prendy, old wine-skin! How are things with you?'

'Admirable,' said Mr Prendergast. 'I have never known them better. I have just caned twenty-three boys.'

CHAPTER XI
Philbrick – continued

NEXT day Mr Prendergast's self-confidence had evaporated.

'Head hurting?' asked Grimes.

'Well, as a matter of fact, it is rather.'

'Eyes tired? Thirsty?'

'Yes, a little.'

'Poor old Prendy! Don't I know? Still, it was worth it, wasn't it?'

'I don't remember very clearly all that happened, but I walked back to the Castle with Philbrick, and he told me all about his life. It appears he is really a rich man and not a butler at all.'

'I know,' said Paul and Grimes simultaneously.

'You both knew? Well, it came as a great surprise to me, although I must admit I had noticed a certain superiority in his manner. But I find almost everyone like that. Did he tell you his whole story – about his shooting the Portuguese Count and everything?'

'No, he didn't tell me *that*,' said Paul.

'Shooting a Portuguese Count? Are you sure you've got hold of the right end of the stick, old boy?'

'Yes, yes, I'm sure of it. It impressed me very much. You see Philbrick is really Sir Solomon Philbrick, the shipowner.'

'The novelist, you mean,' said Grimes.

'The retired burglar,' said Paul.

The three masters looked at each other.

'Old boys, it seems to me someone's been pulling our legs.'

'Well, this is the story that he told me,' continued Mr Prendergast. 'It all started from our argument about Church architecture with the black man. Apparently Philbrick has a large house in Carlton House Terrace.'

'Camberwell Green.'

'Cheyne Walk.'

'Well, I'm telling you what he told me. He has a house in Carlton House Terrace. I remember the address well because a sister of Mrs Crump's was once governess in a house in the same row, and he used to live there with an actress who, I regret to say, was not his wife. I forget her name, but I know it is a particularly famous one. He was sitting in the Athenaeum Club one day when the Archbishop of Canterbury approached him and said that the Government were anxious to make him a peer, but that it was impossible while he lived a life of such open irregularity. Philbrick turned down the offer. He is a Roman Catholic, I forgot to tell you. But all that doesn't really explain why he is here. It only shows how important he is. His ships weigh *hundreds* and *hundreds* of tons, he told me.

'Well, one evening he and his play-actress were giving a party, and they were playing baccarat. There was a Portuguese Count there – a very dark man from the Legation, Philbrick said. The game rapidly became a personal contest between these two. Philbrick won over and over again until the Count had no more money left and had signed many I O U's. Finally, very late in the night, he took from the Countess's hand – she was sitting beside him with haggard eyes watching him play – an enormous emerald. As big as a gold ball, Philbrick said.

' "This has been an heirloom of my family since the first crusade," said the Portuguese Count. "It is the one thing which I had hoped to leave to my poor, poor little son." And he tossed it on to the table.

' "I will wager against it my new four-funnel, turbine-driven liner called *The Queen of Arcady*," said Philbrick.

' "That's not enough," said the Portuguese Countess.

' "And my steam-yacht *Swallow* and four tugs and a coaling-barge,' said Philbrick. All the party rose to applaud his reckless bid.

'The hand was played. Philbrick had won. With a low bow he returned the emerald to the Portuguese Countess. "For your son!" he said. Again the guests applauded, but the Portuguese Count was livid with rage. "You have insulted my honour," he said. "In Portugal we have only one way of dealing with such an occurrence."

'There and then they went out into Hyde Park, which was quite close. They faced each other and fired: it was just dawn. At the feet of the Achilles statue Philbrick shot the Portuguese Count dead. They left him with his smoking revolver in his hand. The Portuguese Countess kissed Philbrick's hand as she entered her car. "No one will ever know," she said. "It will be taken for suicide. It is a secret between us."

'But Philbrick was a changed man. The actress was driven from his house. He fell into a melancholy and paced up and down his deserted home at night, overpowered by his sense of guilt. The Portuguese Countess rang him up, but he told her it was the wrong number. Finally he went to a priest and confessed. He was told that for three years he must give up his house and wealth and live among the lowest of the low. That,' said Mr Prendergast simply, 'is why he is here. Wasn't that the story he told you?'

'No, it wasn't,' said Paul.

'Not the shade of a likeness,' said Grimes. 'He told me all about himself one evening at Mrs Roberts'. It was like this:

'Mr Philbrick, senior, was a slightly eccentric sort of a cove. He made a big pile out of diamond mines while he was quite young and settled in the country and devoted his declining years to literature. He had two kids: Philbrick and a daughter called Gracie. From the start Philbrick was the apple of the old chap's eye, while he couldn't stick Miss Gracie at any price. Philbrick could spout Shakespeare and *Hamlet* and things by the yard before Gracie could read "The cat sat on the mat." When he was eight he had a sonnet printed in the local paper. After that Gracie wasn't in it anywhere. She lived with the servants like Cinderella, Philbrick said, while he, sensible little beggar, had the best of everything and quoted classics and flowery language to the old boy upstairs. After he left Cambridge he settled down in London and wrote away like blazes. The old man just loved that; he had all Philbrick's books bound in blue leather and put in a separate bookcase with a bust of Philbrick on top. Poor old Gracie found things a bit thin, so she ran off with a young chap in the motor trade who didn't know one end of a book from the other, or of a car for that matter, as it turned out. When the old boy popped off he left Philbrick everything, except a few books to Gracie. The young man had only married her because he thought the old boy was bound to leave her something, so he hopped it. That didn't worry Philbrick. He lived for his art, he said. He just moved into a bigger house and went on writing away fifteen to the dozen. Gracie tried to get some money out of him more than once, but he was so busy writing books, he couldn't bother about her. At last she became a cook in a house at Southgate. Next year she died. That didn't worry Philbrick at first. Then after a week or so he noticed an odd thing. There was always a smell of cooking all over the house, in his study, in his bedroom, everywhere. He had an architect in who said he couldn't notice any smell, and rebuilt the kitchen and put in all sorts of ventilators. Still, the smell got worse. It used to hang about his clothes so that he didn't dare go out, a horrible fatty smell. He tried going abroad, but the whole of Paris reeked of English cooking. That was bad enough, but after a time plates began rattling round his bed when he tried to sleep at nights and behind his chair as he wrote his books. He used to wake up in the night and hear the frizzling of fried fish and the singing of kettles. Then he knew what it was: it was Gracie haunting him. He went to the Society for Psychical Research, and they got through a conversation to Gracie. He asked how he could make reparation. She said that he must live among servants for a year and write a book about them that would improve their lot. He tried to go the whole hog at first and started as *chef*, but of course that wasn't really in his line, and the family he was with got so ill, he had to leave. So he came here. He says the book is most moving, and that he'll read me bits of it some day. Not quite the same story as Prendy's.'

'No, it's not. By the way, did he say anything about marrying Dingy?'

'Not a word. He said that as soon as the smell of cooking wore off he was going to be the happiest man in the world. Apparently he's engaged to a female poet in Chelsea. He's not the sort of cove I'd have chosen for a brother-in-law. But then Flossie isn't really the sort of wife I'd have chosen. These things happen, old boy.'

Paul told them about the 'Lamb and Flag' at Camberwell Green and about Toby Cruttwell. 'D'you think that story is true, or yours, or Prendy's?' he asked.

'No,' said Mr Prendergast.

CHAPTER XII
The Agony of Captain Grimes

TWO days later Beste-Chetwynde and Paul were in the organ-loft of the Llanabba Parish Church.

'I don't think I played that terribly well, do you, sir?'

'No.'

'Shall I stop for a bit?'

'I wish you would.'

'Tangent's foot has swollen up and turned black,' said Beste-Chetwynde with relish.

'Poor little brute!' said Paul.

'I had a letter from my mamma this morning,' Beste-Chetwynde went on. 'There's a message for you in it. Shall I read you what she says?'

He took out a letter written on the thickest possible paper. 'The first part is all about racing and a row she's had with Chokey. Apparently he doesn't like the way she's rebuilt our house in the country. I think it was time she dropped that man, don't you?'

'What does she say about me?' asked Paul.

'She says: "*By the way, dear boy, I must tell you that the spelling in your last letters has been* just too shattering *for words. You know how terribly anxious I am for you to get on and go to Oxford, and everything, and I have been thinking, don't you think it might be a good thing if we were to have a tutor next holidays? Would you think it too boring? Some one young who would fit in. I thought, would that good-looking young master you said you liked care to come? How much ought I to pay him? I never know these things. I don't mean the drunk one, tho' he was sweet too.*" I think that must be you, don't you?' said Beste-Chetwynde; 'it can hardly be Captain Grimes.'

'Well, I must think that over,' said Paul. 'It sounds rather a good idea.'

'Well, yes,' said Beste-Chetwynde doubtfully, 'it might be all right, only there mustn't be too much of the schoolmaster about it. That man Prendergast beat me the other evening.'

'And there'll be no organ lessons, either,' said Paul.

Grimes did not receive the news as enthusiastically as Paul had hoped; he was sitting over the Common Room fire despondently biting his nails.

'Good, old boy! That's splendid,' he said abstractedly. 'I'm glad; I am really.'

'Well, you don't sound exactly gay.'

'No, I'm not. Fact is, I'm in the soup again.'

'Badly?'

'Up to the neck.'

'My dear chap, I *am* sorry. What are you going to do about it?'

'I've done the only thing: I've announced my engagement.'

'That'll please Flossie.'

'Oh, yes, she's as pleased as hell about it, damn her nasty little eyes.'

'What did the old man say?'

'Baffled him a bit, old boy. He's just thinking things out at the moment. Well, I expect everything'll be all right.'

'I don't see why it shouldn't be.'

'Well, there *is* a reason. I don't think I told you before, but fact is, I'm married already.'

That evening Paul received a summons from the Doctor. He wore a double-breasted dinner-jacket, which he smoothed uneasily over his hips at Paul's approach. He looked worried and old.

'Pennyfeather,' he said, 'I have this morning received a severe shock, two shocks in fact. The first was disagreeable, but not wholly unexpected. Your colleague, Captain Grimes, has been convicted before me, on evidence that leaves no possibility of his innocence, of a crime – I might almost call it a course of action – which I can neither understand nor excuse. I daresay I need not particularize. However, that is all a minor question. I have quite frequently met with similar cases during a long experience in our profession. But what has disturbed and grieved me more than I can moderately express is the information that he is engaged to be married to my elder daughter. That, Pennyfeather, I had not expected. In the circumstances it seemed a humiliation I might reasonably have been spared. I tell you all this, Pennyfeather, because in our brief acquaintance I have learned to trust and respect you.'

The Doctor sighed, drew from his pocket a handkerchief of *crêpe de chine*, blew his nose with every accent of emotion, and resumed:

'He is *not* the son-in-law I should readily have chosen. I could have forgiven him his wooden leg, his slavish poverty, his moral turpitude, and his abominable features; I could even have forgiven him his incredible vocabulary, if only he had been a *gentleman*. I hope you do not think me a snob. You may have discerned in me a certain prejudice against the lower orders. It is quite true. I *do* feel deeply on the subject. You see, I married one of them. But that, unfortunately, is neither here nor there. What I really wished to say to you was this: I have spoken to the unhappy young woman my daughter, and find that she has no particular inclination towards Grimes. Indeed, I do not think that any daughter of mine could fall as low as that. But she is, for some reason, uncontrollably eager to be married to somebody fairly soon. Now, I should be quite prepared to offer a partnership in Llanabba to a son-in-law of whom I approved. The income of the school is normally not less than three thousand a year – that is with the help of dear Diana's housekeeping – and my junior partner would start at an income of a thousand, and of course succeed to a larger share upon my death. It is a prospect that many young men would find inviting. And I was wondering, Pennyfeather, whether by any chance, looking at the matter from a business-like point of view, without prejudice, you understand, fair and square, taking things as they are for what they are worth, facing facts, whether possibly *you* . . . I wonder if I make myself plain?'

'No,' said Paul. 'No, sir, I'm afraid it would be impossible. I hope I don't appear rude, but – no, really I'm afraid . . . '

'That's all right, my dear boy. Not another word! I quite understand. I was afraid that would be your answer. Well, it must be Grimes, then. I don't think it would be any use approaching Mr Prendergast.'

'It was very kind of you to suggest it, sir.'

'Not at all, not at all. The wedding shall take place a week to-day. You might tell Grimes that if you see him. I don't want to have more to do with him than I can help. I wonder whether it would be a good thing to give a small party?' For a moment a light sprang up in Dr Fagan's eyes and then died out. 'No, no, there will be no party. The sports were not encouraging. Poor little Lord Tangent is still laid up, I hear.'

Paul returned to the Common Room with the Doctor's message.

'Hell!' said Grimes. 'I still hoped it might fall through.'

'What d'you want for a wedding present?' Paul asked.

Grimes brightened. 'What about that binge you promised me and Prendy?'

'All right!' said Paul. 'We'll have it tomorrow.'

*

The Hotel Metropole, Cwmpryddyg, is by far the grandest hotel in the north of Wales. It is situated on a high and healthy eminence overlooking the strip of water that railway companies have gallantly compared to the Bay of Naples. It was built in the ample days preceding the war, with a lavish expenditure on looking-glass and marble. To-day it shows signs of wear, for it has never been quite as popular as its pioneers hoped. There are cracks in the cement on the main terrace, the winter garden is draughty, and one comes disconcertingly upon derelict bathchairs in the Moorish Court. Besides this, none of the fountains ever play, the string band that used to perform nightly in the ballroom has given place to a very expensive wireless set which one of the waiters knows how to operate, there is never any notepaper in the writing-room, and the sheets are not long enough for the beds. Philbrick pointed out these defects to Paul as he sat with Grimes and Mr Prendergast drinking cocktails in the Palm Court before dinner.

'And it isn't as though it was really cheap,' he said. Philbrick had become quite genial during the last few days. 'Still, one can't expect much in Wales, and it is something. I can't live without some kind of luxury for long. I'm not staying this evening, or I'd ask you fellows to dine with me.'

'Philbrick, old boy,' said Grimes, 'me and my pals here have been wanting a word with you for some time. How about those yarns you spun about your being a shipowner and a novelist and a burglar?'

'Since you mention it,' said Philbrick with dignity, 'they were untrue. One day you shall know my full story. It is stranger than any fiction. Meanwhile I have to be back at the Castle. Good night.'

'He certainly seems quite a swell here,' said Grimes as they watched him disappear into the night escorted with every obsequy by the manager and the head-waiter. 'I daresay he *could* tell a story if he wanted to.'

'I believe it's their keys,' said Mr Prendergast suddenly. It was the first time that he had spoken. For twenty minutes he had been sitting very upright in his gilt chair and very alert, his eyes unusually bright, darting this way and that in his eagerness to miss nothing of the gay scene about him.

'What's their keys, Prendy?'

'Why, the things they get given at the counter. I thought for a long time it was money.'

'Is that what's been worrying you? Bless your heart, I thought it was the young lady in the office you were after.'

'Oh, Grimes!' said Mr Prendergast, and he blushed warmly and gave a little giggle.

Paul led his guests into the dining-room.

'I haven't taught French for nothing all these years,' said Grimes, studying the menu. 'I'll start with some jolly old *huîtres*.'

Mr Prendergast ate a grape-fruit with some difficulty. 'What a big orange!' he said when he had finished it. 'They do things on a large scale here.'

The soup came in little aluminium bowls. 'What price the ancestral silver?' said Grimes. The Manchester merchants on the spree who sat all round them began to look a little askance at Paul's table.

'Someone's doing himself well on bubbly,' said Grimes as a waiter advanced staggering under the weight of an ice-pail from which emerged a Jeroboam of champagne. 'Good egg! It's coming to us.'

'With Sir Solomon Philbrick's compliments to Captain Grimes and congratulations on his approaching marriage, sir.'

Grimes took the waiter by the sleeve. 'See here, old boy, this Sir Solomon Philbrick – know him well?'

'He's here quite frequently, sir.'

'Spends a lot of money, eh?'

'He doesn't entertain at all, but he always has the best of everything himself, sir.'

'Does he pay his bill?'

'I really couldn't say, I'm afraid, sir. Would you be requiring anything else?'

'All right, old boy! Don't get sniffy. Only he's a pal of mine, see?'

'Really, Grimes,' said Mr Prendergast, 'I am afraid you made him quite annoyed with your questions, and that stout man over there is staring at us in the most marked way.'

'I've got a toast to propose. Prendy, fill up your glass. Here's to Trumpington, whoever he is, who gave us the money for this binge!'

'And here's to Philbrick,' said Paul, 'whoever *he* is!'

'And here's to Miss Fagan,' said Mr Prendergast, 'with our warmest hopes for her future happiness!'

'Amen,' said Grimes.

After the soup the worst sort of sole. Mr Prendergast made a little joke about soles and souls. Clearly the dinner-party was being a great success.

'You know,' said Grimes, 'look at it how you will, marriage is rather a grim thought.'

'The three reasons for it given in the Prayer-Book have always seemed to me quite inadequate,' agreed Mr Prendergast. 'I have never had the smallest difficulty about the avoidance of fornication, and the other two advantages seem to me nothing short of disastrous.'

'My first marriage,' said Grimes, 'didn't make much odds either way. It was in Ireland. I was tight at the time, and so was everyone else. God knows what became of Mrs Grimes. It seems to me, though, that with Flossie I'm in for a pretty solemn solemnization. It's not what I should have chosen for myself, not by a long chalk. Still, as things are, I suppose it's the best thing that could have happened. I think I've about run through the schoolmastering profession. I don't mind telling you I might have found it pretty hard to get another job. There are limits. Now I'm set up for life, and no more worry about testimonials. That's something. In fact, that's all there is to be said. But there have been moments in the last twenty-four hours, I don't mind telling you, when I've gone cold all over at the thought of what I was in for.'

'I don't want to say anything discouraging,' said Mr Prendergast, 'but I've known Flossie for nearly ten years now, and – '

'There isn't anything you can tell me about Flossie that I don't know already. I almost wish it was Dingy. I suppose it's too late now to change. Oh dear!' said Grimes despondently, gazing into his glass. 'Oh, Lord! oh, Lord! That I should come to this!'

'Cheer up, Grimes. It isn't like you to be as depressed as this,' said Paul.

'Old friends,' said Grimes – and his voice was charged with emotion – 'you see a man standing face to face with retribution. Respect him even if you cannot understand. Those that live by the flesh shall perish by the flesh. I am a very sinful man, and I am past my first youth. Who shall pity me in that dark declivity to which my steps inevitably seem to tend? I have boasted in my youth and held my head high and gone on my way careless of consequence, but ever behind me, unseen, stood stark Justice with his two-edged sword.'

More food was brought them. Mr Prendergast ate with a hearty appetite.

'Oh, why did nobody warn me?' cried Grimes in his agony. 'I should have been told. They should have told me in so many words. They should have warned me about Flossie, not about the fires of hell. I've risked them, and I don't mind risking them again, but they should have told me about marriage. They should have told me that at the end of that gay journey and flower-strewn path were the hideous lights of home and the voices of children. I should have been warned of the great lavender-scented bed that was laid out for me, of the wisteria at the windows, of all the intimacy and confidence of family life. But I daresay I shouldn't have listened. Our life is lived between two homes. We emerge for a little into the light, and then the front door closes. The chintz curtains shut out the sun, and the hearth glows with the fire of home, while upstairs, above our heads, are enacted again the awful accidents of adolescence. There's a home and family waiting for every one of us. We can't escape, try how we may. It's the seed of life we carry about with us like our skeletons, each one of us unconsciously pregnant with desirable villa residences. There's no escape. As individuals we simply do not exist. We are just potential home-builders, beavers, and ants. How do we come into being? What is birth?'

'I've often wondered,' said Mr Prendergast.

'What is this impulse of two people to build their beastly home? It's you and me, unborn, asserting our presence. All we are is a manifestation of the impulse of family life, and if by chance we have escaped the itch ourselves, Nature forces it upon us another way. Flossie's got that itch enough for two. I just haven't. I'm one of the blind alleys off the main road of procreation, but it doesn't matter. Nature always wins. Oh, Lord! oh, Lord! Why didn't I die in that first awful home? Why did I ever hope I could escape?'

Captain Grimes continued his lament for some time in deep bitterness of heart. Presently he became silent and stared at his glass.

'I wonder,' said Mr Prendergast, 'I wonder whether I could have just a little more of this very excellent pheasant?'

'Anyway,' said Grimes, 'there shan't be any children; I'll see to that.'

'It has always been a mystery to me why people marry,' said Mr Prendergast. 'I can't see the smallest reason for it. Quite happy, normal people. Now I can understand it in Grimes' case. He has everything to gain by the arrangement, but what does Flossie expect to gain? And yet she seems more enthusiastic about it than Grimes. It has been the tragedy of my life that whenever I start thinking about any quite simple subject I invariably feel myself confronted by some flat contradiction of this sort. Have you ever thought about marriage – in the abstract, I mean, of course?'

'Not very much, I'm afraid.'

'I don't believe,' said Mr Prendergast, 'that people would ever fall in love or want to be married if they hadn't been told about it. It's like abroad: no one would want to go there if they hadn't been told it existed. Don't you agree?'

'I don't think you can be quite right,' said Paul; 'you see, animals fall in love quite a lot, don't they?'

'Do they?' said Mr Prendergast. 'I didn't know that. What an extraordinary thing! But then I had an aunt whose cat used to put its paw up to its mouth when it yawned. It's wonderful what animals can be taught. There is a sea-lion at the circus, I saw in the paper, who juggles with an umbrella and two oranges.'

'I know what I'll do,' said Grimes. 'I'll get a motor bicycle.'

This seemed to cheer him up a little. He took another glass of wine and smiled wanly. 'I'm afraid I've not been following all you chaps have said. I was thinking. What were we talking about?'

'Prendy was telling me about a sea-lion who juggled with an umbrella and two oranges.'

'Why, that's nothing. I can juggle with a whacking great bottle and a lump of ice and two knives. Look!'

'Grimes, don't! Everyone is looking at you.'

The head-waiter came over to remonstrate. 'Please remember where you are, sir,' he said.

'I know where I am well enough,' said Grimes. 'I'm in the hotel my pal Sir Solomon Philbrick is talking of buying, and

I tell you this, old boy: if he does, the first person to lose his job will be you. See?'

Nevertheless he stopped juggling, and Mr Prendergast ate two *pêches Melba* undisturbed.

'The black cloud has passed,' said Grimes. 'Grimes is now going to enjoy his evening.'

CHAPTER XIII
The Passing of a Public School Man

SIX days later the school was given a half-holiday, and soon after luncheon the bigamous union of Captain Edgar Grimes and Miss Florence Selina Fagan was celebrated at the Llanabba Parish Church. A slight injury to his hand prevented Paul from playing the organ. He walked down the church with Mr Prendergast, who, greatly to his dismay, had been instructed by Dr Fagan to give away the bride.

'I do not intend to be present,' said the Doctor. 'The whole business is exceedingly painful to me.' Everybody else, however, was there except little Lord Tangent, whose foot was being amputated at a local nursing-home. The boys for the most part welcomed the event as a pleasant variation to the rather irregular routine of their day. Clutterbuck alone seemed disposed to sulk.

'I don't suppose that their children will be terribly attractive,' said Beste-Chetwynde.

There were few wedding presents. The boys had subscribed a shilling each and had bought at a shop in Llandudno a silver-plated teapot, coyly suggestive of *art nouveau*. The Doctor gave them a cheque for twenty-five pounds. Mr Prendergast gave Grimes a walking-stick – 'because he was always borrowing mine' – and Dingy, rather generously, two photograph frames, a calendar, and a tray of Benares brassware. Paul was the best man.

The service passed off without a hitch, for Grimes' Irish wife did not turn up to forbid the banns. Flossie wore a frock of a rather noticeable velveteen and a hat with two pink feathers to match.

'I was so pleased when I found he didn't want me to wear white,' she said, 'though, of course, it might have been dyed afterwards.'

Both bride and bridegroom spoke up well in the responses, and afterwards the Vicar delivered a very moving address on the subject of Home and Conjugal Love.

'How beautiful it is,' he said, 'to see two young people in the hope of youth setting out with the Church's blessing to face life together; how much more beautiful to see them when they have grown to full manhood and womanhood coming together and saying, "Our experience of life has taught us that *one* is not enough." '

The boys lined the path from the church door to the lychgate, and the head prefect said: 'Three cheers for Captain and Mrs Grimes!'

Then they returned to the Castle. The honeymoon had been postponed until the end of term, ten days later, and the arrangements for the first days of their married life were a little meagre. 'You must do the best you can,' the Doctor had said. 'I suppose you will wish to share the same bedroom. I think there would be no objection to your both moving into the large room in the West Tower. It is a little damp, but I daresay Diana will arrange for a fire to be lighted there. You may use the morning-room in the evenings, and Captain Grimes will, of course, have his meals at my table in the dining-room, not with the boys. I do not wish to find him sitting about in the drawing-room, nor, of course, in my library. He had better keep his books and gown in the Common Room, as before. Next term I will consider some other arrangement. Perhaps I could hand over one of the lodges to you or fit up some sort of sitting-room in the tower. I was not prepared for a domestic upheaval.'

Diana, who was really coming out of the business rather creditably, put a bowl of flowers in their bedroom, and lit a fire of reckless proportions, in which she consumed the remains of a desk and two of the boys' play-boxes.

That evening, while Mr Prendergast was taking Prep. at the end of the passage, Grimes visited Paul in the Common Room. He looked rather uncomfortable in his evening clothes.

'Well, dinner's over,' he said. 'The old man does himself pretty well.'

'How are you feeling?'

'Not too well, old boy. The first days are always a strain, they say, even in the most romantic marriages. My father-in-law is *not* what you might call easy. Needs thawing gently, you know. I suppose as a married man I oughtn't to go down to Mrs Roberts'?'

'I think it might seem odd on the first evening, don't you?'

'Flossie's playing the piano; Dingy's making up the accounts; the old man's gone off to the library. Don't you think we've time for a quick one?'

Arm in arm they went down the familiar road.

'Drinks are on me to-night,' said Grimes.

The silver band were still sitting with their heads together discussing the division of their earnings.

'They tell me that married this afternoon you were?' said the stationmaster.

'That's right,' said Grimes.

'And my sister-in-law never at all you would meet whatever,' he continued reproachfully.

'Look here, old boy,' said Grimes, 'just you shut up. You're not being tactful. See? Just you keep quiet, and I'll give you all some nice beer.'

When Mrs Roberts shut her doors for the night, Paul and Grimes turned back up the hill. A light was burning in the West Tower.

'There she is, waiting for me,' said Grimes. 'Now it might be a very romantic sight to some chaps, a light burning in a tower window. I knew a poem about a thing like that once. Forget it now, though. I was no end of a one for poetry when I was a kid – love and all that. Castle towers came in quite a lot. Funny how one grows out of that sort of thing.'

Inside the Castle he turned off down the main corridor.

'Well, so long, old boy! This is the way I go now. See you in the morning.' The baize door swung to behind him, and Paul went up to bed.

*

Paul saw little of Grimes during the next few days. They met at prayers and on the way to and from their classrooms, but the baize door that separated the school from the Doctor's wing was also separating them. Mr Prendergast, now in unchallenged possession of the other easy-chair, was smoking away one evening when he suddenly said:

'You know, I miss Grimes. I didn't think I should, but I do. With all his faults, he was a very cheery person. I think I was beginning to get on better with him.'

'He doesn't look as cheery as he did,' said Paul. 'I don't believe that life "above stairs" is suiting him very well.'

As it happened, Grimes chose that evening to visit them.

'D'you chaps mind if I come in for a bit?' he asked with unwonted diffidence. They rose to welcome him. 'Sure you don't mind? I won't stay long.'

'My dear man, we were just saying how much we missed you. Come and sit down.'

'Won't you have some of my tobacco?' said Prendergast.

'Thanks, Prendy! I just had to come in and have a chat. I've been feeling pretty fed up lately. Married life is *not* all beer and skittles, I don't mind telling you. It's not Flossie, mind; she's been hardly any trouble at all. In a way I've got quite to like her. She likes me, anyway, and that's the great thing. The Doctor's my trouble. He never lets me alone, that man. It gets on my nerves. Always laughing at me in a nasty kind of way and making me feel small. You know the way Lady Circumference talks to the Clutterbucks – like that. I tell you I simply dread going into meals in that dining-room. He's got a sort of air as though he always knew exactly what I was going to say before I said it, and as if it was always a little worse than he'd expected. Flossie says he treats *her* that way sometimes. He does it to me the whole time, damn him.'

'I don't expect he means it,' said Paul, 'and anyway I shouldn't bother about it.'

'That's the point. I'm beginning to feel he's quite right. I suppose I am a pretty coarse sort of chap. I don't know anything about art, and I haven't met any grand people, and I don't go to a good tailor, and all that. I'm not what he calls "out of the top drawer". I never pretended I was, but the thing is that up till now it hasn't worried me. I don't think I was a conceited sort of chap, but I felt as good as anyone else, and I didn't care what people thought as long as I had my fun. And I *did* have fun, too, and, what's more, I enjoyed it. But now I've lived with that man for a week, I feel quite different. I feel half ashamed of myself all the time. And I've come to recognize that supercilious look he gives me in other people's eyes as well.'

'Ah, how well I know that feeling!' sighed Mr Prendergast.

'I used to think I was popular among the boys, but you know I'm not, and at Mrs Roberts' they only pretend to like me in the hope I'd stand 'em drinks. I did, too, but they never gave me one back. I thought it was just because they were Welsh, but I see now it was because they despised me. I don't blame them. God knows I despise myself. You know, I used to use French phrases a certain amount – things like *savoir faire* and *Je ne sais quoi*. I never thought about it, but I suppose I haven't got much of an accent. How could I? I've never been in France except for that war. Well, every time I say one of them now the Doctor gives a sort of wince as if he's bitten on a bad tooth. I have to think the whole time now before I say anything, to see if there's any French in it or any of the expressions he doesn't think refined. Then when I do say anything my voice sounds so funny that I get in a muddle and he winces again. Old boy, it's been hell this last week, and it's worrying me. I'm getting an inferiority complex. Dingy's like that. She just never speaks now. He's always making little jokes about Flossie's clothes, too, but I don't think the old girl sees what he's driving at. That man'll have me crazy before the term's over.'

'Well, there's only a week more,' was all that Paul could say to comfort him.

*

Next morning at prayers Grimes handed Paul a letter. 'Irony,' he said.

Paul opened it and read:

> *John Clutterbuck & Sons,*
> *Wholesale Brewers and Wine Merchants.*

My Dear Grimes,

The other day at the sports you asked whether there was by any chance a job open for you at the brewery. I don't know if you were serious in this, but if you were a post has just fallen vacant which I feel might suit you. I should be glad to offer it to any friend who has been so kind to Percy. We employ a certain number of travellers to go round to various inns and hotels to sample the beer and see that it has not been diluted or in any way adulterated. Our junior traveller, who was a friend of mine from Cambridge, had just developed D.T.'s and has had to be suspended. The salary is two hundred a year with car and travelling expenses. Would this attract you at all? If so, will you let me know during the next few days.

> *Yours sincerely,*
> *Sam Clutterbuck.*

'Just look at that,' said Grimes. 'God's own job and mine for the asking! If that had come ten days ago my whole life might have been different.'

'You don't think of taking it now?'

'Too late, old boy, too late. The saddest words in the English language.'

In 'break' Grimes said to Paul: 'Look here, I've decided to take Sam Clutterbuck's job, and be damned to the Fagans!' His eyes shone with excitement. 'I shan't say a word to them.

I shall just go off. They can do what they like about it. I don't care.'

'Splendid!' said Paul. 'It's much the best thing you can do.'

'I'm going this very afternoon,' said Grimes.

An hour later, at the end of morning school, they met again. 'I've been thinking over that letter,' said Grimes. 'I see it all now. It's just a joke.'

'Nonsense!' said Paul. 'I'm sure it isn't. Go and see the Clutterbucks right away.'

'No, no, they don't mean it seriously. They've heard about my marriage from Percy, and they're just pulling my leg. It was too good to be true. Why should they offer *me* a job like that, even if such a wonderful job exists?'

'My dear Grimes, I'm perfectly certain it was a genuine offer. Anyway, there's nothing to lose by going to see them.'

'No, no, it's too late, old boy. Things like that don't happen.' And he disappeared beyond the baize door.

*

Next day there was fresh trouble at Llanabba. Two men in stout boots, bowler hats, and thick grey overcoats presented themselves at the Castle with a warrant for Philbrick's arrest. Search was made for him, but it was suddenly discovered that he had already left by the morning train for Holyhead. The boys crowded round the detectives with interest and a good deal of disappointment. They were not, they thought, particularly impressive figures as they stood in the hall fingering their hats and drinking whisky and calling Dingy 'miss'.

'We've been after 'im for some time now,' said the first detective. 'Ain't we, Bill?'

'Pretty near six months. It's too bad, his getting away like this. They're getting rather restless at H.Q. about our travelling expenses.'

'Is it a very serious case?' asked Mr Prendergast. The entire school were by this time assembled in the hall. 'Not shooting or anything like that?'

'No, there ain't been no bloodshed up to date, sir. I oughtn't to tell about it, really, but seeing as you've all been mixed up in it to some extent, I don't mind telling you that I think he'll get off on a plea of insanity. Loopy, you know.'

'What's he been up to?'

'False pretences and impersonation, sir. There's five charges against him in different parts of the country, mostly at hotels. He represents himself as a rich man, stays there for some time living like a lord, cashes a big cheque and then goes off. Calls 'isself Sir Solomon Philbrick. Funny thing is, I think he really believes his tale 'isself. I've come across several cases like that one time or another. There was a bloke in Somerset what thought 'e was Bishop of Bath and Wells and confirmed a whole lot of kids – very reverent, too.'

'Well, anyway,' said Dingy, 'he went without his wages from here.'

'I always felt there was something untrustworthy about that man,' said Mr Prendergast.

'Lucky devil!' said Grimes despondently.

*

'I'm worried about Grimes,' said Mr Prendergast that evening. 'I never saw a man more changed. He used to be so self-confident and self-assertive. He came in here quite timidly just now and asked me whether I believed that Divine retribution took place in this world or the next. I began to talk to him about it, but I could see he wasn't listening. He sighed once or twice and then went out without a word while I was still speaking.'

'Beste-Chetwynde tells me he has kept in the whole of the third form because the blackboard fell down in his classroom this morning. He was convinced they had arranged it on purpose.'

'Yes, they often do.'

'But in this case, they hadn't. Beste-Chetwynde said they were quite frightened at the way he spoke to them. Just like an actor, Beste-Chetwynde said.'

'Poor Grimes! I think he is seriously unnerved. It will be a relief when the holidays come.'

But Captain Grimes' holiday came sooner than Mr Prendergast expected, and in a way which few people could have foreseen. Three days later he did not appear at morning prayers, and Flossie, red-eyed, admitted that he had not come in from the village the night before. Mr Davies, the stationmaster, confessed to seeing him earlier in the evening in a state of depression. Just before luncheon a youth presented himself at the Castle with a little pile of clothes he had found on the seashore. They were identified without difficulty as having belonged to the Captain. In the breast pocket of the jacket was an envelope addressed to the Doctor, and in it a slip of paper inscribed with the words: 'THOSE THAT LIVE BY THE FLESH SHALL PERISH BY THE FLESH.'

As far as was possible this intelligence was kept from the boys.

Flossie, though severely shocked at this untimely curtailment of her married life, was firm in her resolution not to wear mourning. 'I don't think my husband would have expected it of me,' she said.

In these distressing circumstances the boys began packing their boxes to go away for the Easter holidays.

END OF PART ONE

PART TWO

CHAPTER I
King's Thursday

MARGOT BESTE-CHETWYNDE had two houses in England
– one in London and the other in Hampshire. Her London
house, built in the reign of William and Mary, was, by
universal consent, the most beautiful building between Bond
Street and Park Lane, but opinion was divided on the subject
of her country house. This was very new indeed; in fact, it
was scarcely finished when Paul went to stay there at the
beginning of the Easter holidays. No single act in Mrs Beste-
Chetwynde's eventful and in many ways disgraceful career had
excited quite so much hostile comment as the building, or
rather the rebuilding, of this remarkable house.

It was called King's Thursday, and stood on the place which
since the reign of Bloody Mary had been the seat of the Earls
of Pastmaster. For three centuries the poverty and inertia of
this noble family had preserved its home unmodified by any
of the succeeding fashions that fell upon domestic architecture.
No wing had been added, no window filled in; no portico,
façade, terrace, orangery, tower, or battlement marred its
timbered front. In the craze for coal-gas and indoor sanitation,
King's Thursday had slept unscathed by plumber or engineer.
The estate carpenter, an office hereditary in the family of the
original joiner who had panelled the halls and carved the great
staircase, did such restorations as became necessary from time
to time for the maintenance of the fabric, working with the
same tools and with the traditional methods, so that in a few
years his work became indistinguishable from that of his grand-
sires. Rushlights still flickered in the bedrooms long after all
Lord Pastmaster's neighbours were blazing away electricity,

and in the last fifty years Hampshire had gradually become proud of King's Thursday. From having been considered rather a blot on the progressive county, King's Thursday gradually became the Mecca of week-end parties. 'I thought we might go over to tea at the Pastmasters',' hostesses would say after luncheon on Sundays. 'You really must see their house. Quite unspoilt, my dear. Professor Franks, who was here last week, said it was recognized as the finest piece of domestic Tudor in England.'

It was impossible to ring the Pastmasters up, but they were always at home and unaffectedly delighted to see their neighbours, and after tea Lord Pastmaster would lead the newcomers on a tour round the house, along the great galleries and into the bedrooms, and would point out the priest-hole and the closet where the third Earl imprisoned his wife for wishing to rebuild a smoking chimney. 'That chimney still smokes when the wind's in the east,' he would say, 'but we haven't rebuilt it yet.'

Later they would drive away in their big motor cars to their modernized manors, and as they sat in their hot baths before dinner the more impressionable visitors might reflect how they seemed to have been privileged to step for an hour and a half out of their own century into the leisurely, prosaic life of the English Renaissance, and how they had talked at tea of field-sports and the reform of the Prayer-Book just as the very-great-grandparents of their host might have talked in the same chairs and before the same fire three hundred years before, when their own ancestors, perhaps, slept on straw or among the aromatic merchandise of some Hanse ghetto.

But the time came when King's Thursday had to be sold. It had been built in an age when twenty servants were not an unduly extravagant establishment, and it was scarcely possible to live there with fewer. But servants, the Beste-Chetwyndes found, were less responsive than their masters to the charms of Tudor simplicity; the bedrooms originally ordained for them among the maze of rafters that supported the arches of uneven stone roofs were unsuited to modern requirements, and only the dirtiest and most tipsy of cooks could be induced to inhabit the enormous stone-flagged kitchen or turn the spits at the open fire. Housemaids tended to melt away under the recurring strain of trotting in the bleak hour before breakfast up and down the narrow servants' staircases and along the interminable passages with jugs of warm water for the morning baths. Modern democracy called for lifts and labour-saving devices, for hot-water taps and cold-water taps and (horrible innovation!) drinking water taps, for gas-rings, and electric ovens.

With rather less reluctance than might have been expected, Lord Pastmaster made up his mind to sell the house; to tell the truth, he could never quite see what all the fuss was about; he supposed it was very historic, and all that, but his own taste lay towards the green shutters and semi-tropical vegetation of a villa on the French Riviera, in which, if his critics had only realized it, he was fulfilling the traditional character of his family far better than by struggling on at King's Thursday. But the County was slow to observe this, and something very like consternation was felt, not only in the Great Houses, but in the bungalows and the villas for miles about, while in the neighbouring rectories antiquarian clergymen devised folk-tales of the disasters that should come to crops and herds when there was no longer a Beste-Chetwynde at King's Thursday. Mr Jack Spire in the *London Hercules* wrote eloquently on the *Save King's Thursday Fund*, urging that it should be preserved for the nation, but only a very small amount was collected of the very large sum which Lord Pastmaster was sensible enough to demand, and the theory that it was to be transplanted and re-erected in Cincinnati found wide acceptance.

Thus the news that Lord Pastmaster's rich sister-in-law had bought the family seat was received with the utmost delight by her new neighbours and by Mr Jack Spire, and all sections of the London Press which noticed the sale. *Teneat Bene Beste-Chetwynde*, the motto carved over the chimneypiece in the great hall, was quoted exultantly on all sides, for very little was known about Margot Beste-Chetwynde in Hampshire, and the illustrated papers were always pleased to take any occasion to embellish their pages with her latest portrait; the reporter to whom she remarked, 'I can't think of anything more bourgeois and awful than timbered Tudor architecture,' did not take in what she meant or include the statement in his 'story'.

King's Thursday had been empty for two years when Margot Beste-Chetwynde bought it. She had been there once before, during her engagement.

'It's worse than I thought, far worse,' she said as she drove up the main avenue which the loyal villagers had decorated with the flags of the sometime allied nations in honour of her arrival. 'Liberty's new building cannot be compared with it,' she said, and stirred impatiently in the car, as she remembered, how many years ago, the romantic young heiress who had walked entranced among the cut yews, and had been wooed, how phlegmatically, in the odour of honeysuckle.

Mr Jack Spire was busily saving St Sepulchre's, Egg Street (where Dr Johnson is said once to have attended Matins), when Margot Beste-Chetwynde's decision to rebuild King's Thursday became public. He said, very seriously: 'Well, we did what we could,' and thought no more about it.

Not so the neighbours, who as the work of demolition proceeded, with the aid of all that was most pulverizing in modern machinery, became increasingly enraged, and, in their eagerness to preserve for the county a little of the great manor, even resorted to predatory expeditions, from which they would return with lumps of carved stonework for their rock gardens, until the contractors were forced to maintain an extra watchman at night. The panelling went to South Kensington, where it has come in for a great deal of admiration from the Indian students. Within nine months of Mrs Beste-Chetwynde's taking possession the new architect was at work on his plans.

It was Otto Friedrich Silenus' first important commission. 'Something clean and square,' had been Mrs Beste-Chetwynde's instructions, and then she had disappeared on one of her mysterious world-tours, saying as she left: 'Please see that it is finished by the spring.'

Professor Silenus – for that was the title by which this extraordinary young man chose to be called – was a 'find' of Mrs Beste-Chetwynde's. He was not yet very famous anywhere, though all who met him carried away deep and diverse impressions of his genius. He had first attracted Mrs Beste-Chetwynde's attention with the rejected design for a chewing-gum factory which had been produced in a progressive Hungarian quarterly. His only other completed work was the *décor* for a cinema-film of great length and complexity of plot – a complexity rendered the more inextricable by the producer's austere elimination of all human characters, a fact which had proved fatal to its commercial success. He was starving resignedly in a bed-sitting-room in Bloomsbury, despite the untiring efforts of his parents to find him – they were very rich in Hamburg – when he was offered the commission of rebuilding King's Thursday. 'Something clean and square' – he pondered for three hungry days upon the aesthetic implications of these instructions and then began his designs.

'The problem of architecture as I see it,' he told a journalist who had come to report on the progress of his surprising creation of ferro-concrete and aluminium, 'is the problem of all art – the elimination of the human element from the consideration of form. The only perfect building must be the factory, because that is built to house machines, not men. I do not think it is possible for domestic architecture to be beautiful, but I am doing my best. All ill comes from man,' he said gloomily; 'please tell your readers that. Man is never beautiful, he is never happy except when he becomes the channel for the distribution of mechanical forces.'

The journalist looked doubtful. 'Now, Professor,' he said, 'tell me this. Is it a fact that you have refused to take any fee for the work you are doing, if you don't mind my asking?'

'It is not,' said Professor Silenus.

'Peer's Sister-in-Law Mansion Builder on Future of Architecture,' thought the journalist happily. 'Will machines live in houses? Amazing forecast of Professor-Architect.'

Professor Silenus watched the reporter disappear down the drive and then, taking a biscuit from his pocket, began to munch.

'I suppose there ought to be a staircase,' he said gloomily. 'Why can't the creatures stay in one place? Up and down, in and out, round and round! Why can't they sit still and work? Do dynamos require staircases? Do monkeys require houses? What an immature, self-destructive, antiquated mischief is man! How obscure and gross his prancing and chattering on his little stage of evolution! How loathsome and beyond words boring all the thoughts and self-approval of his biological by-product! this half-formed, ill-conditioned body! this erratic, maladjusted mechanism of his soul: on one side the harmonious instincts and balanced responses of the animal, on the other the inflexible purpose of the engine, and between them man, equally alien from the *being* of Nature and the *doing* of the machine, the vile *becoming!*'

Two hours later the foreman in charge of the concrete-mixer came to consult with the Professor. He had not moved from where the journalist had left him; his fawn-like eyes were fixed and inexpressive, and the hand which had held the biscuit still rose and fell to and from his mouth with a regular motion, while his empty jaws champed rhythmically; otherwise he was wholly immobile.

CHAPTER II
Interlude in Belgravia

ARTHUR POTTS knew all about King's Thursday and Professor Silenus.

On the day of Paul's arrival in London he rang up his old friend and arranged to dine with him at the Queen's Restaurant in Sloane Square. It seemed quite natural that they should be again seated at the table where they had discussed so many subjects of public importance, Budgets and birth control and

Byzantine mosaics. For the first time since the disturbing evening of the Bollinger dinner he felt at ease. Llanabba Castle, with its sham castellations and preposterous inhabitants, had sunk into the oblivion that waits upon even the most lurid of nightmares. Here were sweet corn and pimentoes, and white Burgundy, and the grave eyes of Arthur Potts, and there on the peg over his head hung the black hat he had bought in St James's that afternoon. For an evening at least the shadow that has flitted about this narrative under the name of Paul Pennyfeather materialized into the solid figure of an intelligent, well-educated, well-conducted young man, a man who could be trusted to use his vote at a general election with discretion and proper detachment, whose opinion on a ballet or a critical essay was rather better than most people's, who could order a dinner without embarrassment and in a creditable French accent, who could be trusted to see to luggage at foreign railway-stations and might be expected to acquit himself with decision and decorum in all the emergencies of civilized life. This was the Paul Pennyfeather who had been developing in the placid years which preceded this story. In fact, the whole of this book is really an account of the mysterious disappearance of Paul Pennyfeather, so that readers must not complain if the shadow which took his name does not amply fill the important part of hero for which he was originally cast.

'I saw some of Otto Silenus' work at Munich,' said Potts. 'I think that he's a man worth watching. He was in Moscow at one time and in the Bauhaus at Dessau. He can't be more than twenty-five now. There were some photographs of King's Thursday in a paper the other day. It looked extraordinarily interesting. It's said to be the only really *imaginative* building since the French Revolution. He's got right away from Corbusier, anyway.'

'If people realized,' said Paul, 'Corbusier is a pure nine-teenth-century, Manchester school utilitarian, and that's why they like him.'

Then Paul told Potts about the death of Grimes and the doubts of Mr Prendergast, and Potts told Paul about rather an interesting job he had got under the League of Nations and how he had decided not to take his Schools in consequence and of the unenlightened attitude adopted in the matter by Potts' father.

For an evening Paul became a real person again, but next day he woke up leaving himself disembodied somewhere between Sloane Square and Onslow Square. He had to meet Beste-Chetwynde and catch a morning train to King's Thursday, and there his extraordinary adventures began anew. From the point of view of this story Paul's second disappearance is necessary, because, as the reader will probably have discerned already, Paul Pennyfeather would never have made a hero, and the only interest about him arises from the unusual series of events of which his shadow was witness.

CHAPTER III
Pervigilium Veneris

'I'M looking forward to seeing our new house,' said Beste-Chetwynde as they drove out from the station. 'Mamma says it may be rather a surprise.'

The lodges and gates had been left undisturbed, and the lodge-keeper's wife, white-aproned as Mrs Noah, bobbed at the car as it turned into the avenue. The temperate April sunlight fell through the budding chestnuts and revealed between their trunks green glimpses of parkland and the distant radiance of a lake. 'English spring,' thought Paul. 'In the dreaming ancestral beauty of the English country.' Surely, he thought, these great chestnuts in the morning sun stood for something enduring and serene in a world that had lost its reason and would so stand when the chaos and confusion were forgotten? And surely it was the spirit of William Morris that whispered to him in Margot Beste-Chetwynde's motor car about seed-time and harvest, the superb succession of the seasons, the harmonious interdependence of rich and poor, of dignity, innocence, and tradition? But at a turn in the drive the cadence of his thoughts was abruptly transected. They had come into sight of the house.

'Golly!' said Beste-Chetwynde. 'Mamma has done herself proud this time.'

The car stopped. Paul and Beste-Chetwynde got out, stretched themselves, and were led across a floor of bottle-green glass into the dining-room, where Mrs Beste-Chetwynde was already seated at the vulcanite table beginning her luncheon.

'My dears,' she cried, extending a hand to each of them, 'how divine to see you! I have been waiting for this to go straight to bed.'

She was a thousand times more beautiful than all Paul's feverish recollections of her. He watched her, transported.

'Darling boy, how are you?' she said. 'Do you know you're beginning to look rather lovely in a coltish kind of way. Don't you think so, Otto?'

Paul had noticed nothing in the room except Mrs Beste-Chetwynde; he now saw that there was a young man sitting beside her, with very fair hair and large glasses, behind which his eyes lay like slim fish in an aquarium; they woke from their slumber, flashed iridescent in the light, and darted towards little Beste-Chetwynde.

'His head is too big, and his hands are too small,' said Professor Silenus. 'But his skin is pretty.'

'How would it be if I made Mr Pennyfeather a cocktail?' Beste-Chetwynde asked.

'Yes, Peter, dear, do. He makes them rather well. You can't think what a week I've had, moving in and taking the neighbours round the house and the Press photographers. Otto's house doesn't seem to be a great success with the county, does it, Otto? What was it Lady Vanburgh said?'

'Was that the woman like Napoleon the Great?'

'Yes, darling.'

'She said she understood that the drains were satisfactory, but that, of course, they were underground. I asked her if she wished to make use of them, and said that I did, and went away. But, as a matter of fact, she was quite right. They are the only tolerable part of the house. How glad I shall be when the mosaics are finished and I can go!'

'Don't you like it?' asked Peter Beste-Chetwynde over the cocktail-shaker. 'I think it's so good. It was rather Chokey's taste before.'

'I hate and detest every bit of it,' said Professor Silenus gravely. 'Nothing I have ever done has caused me so much disgust.' With a deep sigh he rose from the table and walked from the room, the fork with which he had been eating still held in his hand.

'Otto has real genius,' said Mrs Beste-Chetwynde. 'You must be sweet to him, Peter. There's a whole lot of people coming down to-morrow for the week-end, and, my dear, that Maltravers has invited himself again. You wouldn't like him for a stepfather, would you, darling?'

'No,' said Peter. 'If you must marry again do choose someone young and quiet.'

'Peter, you're an angel. I will. But now I'm going to bed. I had to wait to see you both. Show Mr Pennyfeather the way about, darling.'

The aluminium lift shot up, and Paul came down to earth.

.'That's an odd thing to ask me in a totally strange house,' said Peter Beste-Chetwynde. 'Anyway, let's have some luncheon.'

It was three days before Paul next saw Mrs Beste-Chetwynde.

*

'Don't you think that she's the most wonderful woman in the world?' said Paul.

'Wonderful? In what way?'

He and Professor Silenus were standing on the terrace after dinner. The half-finished mosaics at their feet were covered with planks and sacking; the great colonnade of black glass pillars shone in the moonlight; beyond the polished aluminium balustrade the park stretched silent and illimitable.

'The most beautiful and the most free. She almost seems like the creature of a different species. Don't you feel that?'

'No,' said the Professor after a few moments' consideration. 'I can't say that I do. If you compare her with other women of her age you will see that the particulars in which she differs from them are infinitesimal compared with the points of similarity. A few millimetres here and a few millimetres there, such variations are inevitable in the human reproductive system; but in all her essential functions – her digestion, for example – she conforms to type.'

'You might say that about anybody.'

'Yes, I do. But it's Margot's variations that I dislike so much. They are small, but obtrusive, like the teeth of a saw. Otherwise I might marry her.'

'Why do you think she would marry you?'

'Because, as I said, all her essential functions are normal. Anyway, she asked me to twice. The first time I said I would think it over, and the second time I refused. I'm sure I was right. She would interrupt me terribly. Besides, she's getting old. In ten years she will be almost worn out.'

Professor Silenus looked at his watch – a platinum disc from Cartier, the gift of Mrs Beste-Chetwynde. 'Quarter to ten,' he said. 'I must go to bed.' He threw the end of his cigar clear of the terrace in a glowing parabola. 'What do you take to make you sleep?'

'I sleep quite easily,' said Paul, 'except on trains.'

'You're lucky. Margot takes veronal. I haven't been to sleep for over a year. That's why I go to bed early. One needs more rest if one doesn't sleep.'

That night as Paul marked his place in *The Golden Bough*, and, switching off his light, turned over to sleep, he thought of the young man a few bedrooms away, lying motionless in the darkness, his hands at his sides, his legs stretched out, his eyes closed, and his brain turning and turning regularly all the night through, drawing in more and more power, storing it away like honey in its intricate cells and galleries, till the atmosphere about it became exhausted and vitiated and only the brain remained turning in the darkness.

So Margot Beste-Chetwynde wanted to marry Otto Silenus, and in another corner of this extraordinary house she lay in a drugged trance, her lovely body cool and fragrant and scarcely stirring beneath the bedclothes; and outside in the park a thousand creatures were asleep, and beyond that, again, were Arthur Potts, and Mr Prendergast, and the Llanabba stationmaster. Quite soon Paul fell asleep. Downstairs Peter Beste-Chetwynde mixed himself another brandy and soda and turned a page in Havelock Ellis, which, next to *The Wind in the Willows*, was his favourite book.

*

The aluminium blinds shot up, and the sun poured in through the vita-glass, filling the room with beneficent rays. Another day had begun at King's Thursday.

From his bathroom window Paul looked down on to the terrace. The coverings had been removed, revealing the half-finished pavement of silver and scarlet. Professor Silenus was already out there directing two workmen with the aid of a chart.

The week-end party arrived at various times in the course of the day, but Mrs Beste-Chetwynde kept to her room while Peter received them in the prettiest way possible. Paul never learned all their names, nor was he ever sure how many of them there were. He supposed about eight or nine, but as they all wore so many different clothes of identically the same kind, and spoke in the same voice, and appeared so irregularly at meals, there may have been several more or several less.

The first to come were The Hon. Miles Malpractice and David Lennox, the photographer. They emerged with little shrieks from an Edwardian electric brougham and made straight for the nearest looking-glass.

In a minute the panotrope was playing, David and Miles were dancing, and Peter was making cocktails. The party had begun. Throughout the afternoon new guests arrived, drifting in vaguely or running in with cries of welcome just as they thought suited them best.

Pamela Popham, square-jawed and resolute as a big-game huntress, stared round the room through her spectacles, drank three cocktails, said: 'My God!' twice, cut two or three of her friends, and stalked off to bed.

'Tell Olivia I've arrived when she comes,' she said to Peter. After dinner they went to a whist drive and dance in the village hall. By half-past two the house was quiet; at half-past three Lord Parakeet arrived, slightly drunk and in evening clothes, having 'just escaped less than one second ago' from Alastair Trumpington's twenty-first birthday party in London.

'Alastair was with me some of the way,' he said, 'but I think he must have fallen out.'

The party, or some of it, reassembled in pyjamas to welcome him. Parakeet walked round bird-like and gay, pointing his thin white nose and making rude little jokes at everyone in turn in a shrill, emasculate voice. At four the house was again at rest.

*

Only one of the guests appeared to be at all ill at ease: Sir Humphrey Maltravers, the Minister of Transportation. He arrived early in the day with a very large car and two very small suitcases, and from the first showed himself as a discordant element in the gay little party by noticing the absence of their hostess.

'Margot? No, I haven't seen her at all. I don't believe she's terribly well,' said one of them, 'or perhaps she's lost somewhere in the house. Peter will know.'

Paul found him seated alone in the garden after luncheon, smoking a large cigar, his big red hands folded before him, a soft hat tilted over his eyes, his big red face both defiant and disconsolate. He bore a preternatural resemblance to his caricatures in the evening papers, Paul thought.

'Hullo, young man!' he said. 'Where's everybody?'

'I think Peter's taking them on a tour round the house. It's much more elaborate than it looks from outside. Would you care to join them?'

'No, thank you, not for me. I came here for a rest. These young people tire me. I have enough of the House during the week.' Paul laughed politely. 'It's the devil of a session. You keen on politics at all?'

'Hardly at all,' Paul said.

'Sensible fellow! I can't think why I keep on at it. It's a dog's life, and there's no money in it, either. If I'd stayed at the Bar I'd have been a rich man by now.

'Rest, rest and riches,' he said − 'it's only after forty one begins to value things of that kind. And half one's life, perhaps, is lived after forty. Solemn thought that. Bear it in mind, young man, and it will save you from most of the worst mistakes. If everyone at twenty realized that half his life was to be lived after forty . . .

'Mrs Beste-Chetwynde's cooking and Mrs Beste-Chetwynde's garden,' said Sir Humphrey meditatively. 'What could be desired more except our fair hostess herself? Have you known her long?'

'Only a few weeks,' said Paul.

'There's no one like her,' said Sir Humphrey. He drew a deep breath of smoke. Beyond the yew hedges the panotrope could be faintly heard. 'What did she want to build this house for?' he asked. 'It all comes of this set she's got into. It's not doing her any good. Damned awkward position to be in − a rich woman without a husband! Bound to get herself talked about. What Margot ought to do is to marry − someone who would stabilize her position, someone,' said Sir Humphrey, 'with a position in public life.'

And then, without any apparent connexion of thought, he began talking about himself. ' "Aim high" has been my motto,' said Sir Humphrey, 'all through my life. You probably won't get what you want, but you may get something; aim low, and you get nothing at all. It's like throwing a stone at a cat. When

I was a kid that used to be great sport in our yard; I daresay you were throwing cricket-balls when you were that age, but it's the same thing. If you throw straight at it, you fall short; aim above, and with luck you score. Every kid knows that. I'll tell you the story of my life.'

Why was it, Paul wondered, that everyone he met seemed to specialize in this form of autobiography? He supposed he must have a sympathetic air. Sir Humphrey told of his early life: of a family of nine living in two rooms, of a father who drank and a mother who had fits, of a sister who went on the streets, of a brother who went to prison, of another brother who was born a deaf-mute. He told of scholarships and poly-technics, of rebuffs and encouragements, of a University career of brilliant success and unexampled privations.

'I used to do proof-reading for the Holywell Press,' he said; 'then I learned shorthand and took down the University ser-mons for the local papers.'

As he spoke the clipped yews seemed to grow grey with the soot of the slums, and the panotrope in the distance took on the gay regularity of a barrel-organ heard up a tenement staircase.

'We were a pretty hot lot at Scone in my time,' he said, naming several high officers of state with easy familiarity, 'but none of them had so far to go as I had.'

Paul listened patiently, as was his habit. Sir Humphrey's words flowed easily, because, as a matter of fact, he was rehearsing a series of articles he had dictated the evening before for publication in a Sunday newspaper. He told Paul about his first briefs and his first general election, the historic Liberal campaign of 1906, and of the strenuous days just before the formation of the Coalition.

'I've nothing to be ashamed of,' said Sir Humphrey. 'I've gone farther than most people. I suppose that, if I keep on, I may one day lead the party. But all this winter I've been feeling that I've got as far as I shall ever get. I've got to the time when I should like to go into the other House and give up work and perhaps keep a racehorse or two' – and his eyes took on the far-away look of a popular actress describing the cottage of her dreams – 'and a yacht and a villa at Monte. The others can do that when they like, and they know it. It's not till you get to my age that you really feel the disadvantage of having been born poor.'

On Sunday evening Sir Humphrey suggested a 'hand of cards'. The idea was received without enthusiasm.

'Wouldn't that be rather *fast*?' said Miles. 'It is Sunday. I think cards are divine, particularly the kings. Such *naughty* old faces! But if I start playing for money, I always lose my temper and cry. Ask Pamela; she's so brave and manly.'

'Let's all play billiards and make a Real House Party of it,' said David, 'or shall we have a Country House Rag?'

'Oh I do feel such a *rip*,' said Miles when he was at last persuaded to play. Sir Humphrey won. Parakeet lost thirty pounds, and opening his pocket book, paid him in ten-pound notes.

'How he did cheat!' said Olivia on the way to bed.

'Did he, darling? Well, let's *jolly well* not pay him,' said Miles.

'It never occurred to me to do such a thing. Why, I couldn't afford to possibly.'

Peter tossed Sir Humphrey double or quits, and won.

'After all, I am host,' he explained.

'When I was your age,' said Sir Humphrey to Miles, 'we used to sit up all night sometimes playing poker. Heavy money, too.'

'Oh, you wicked old thing!' said Miles.

Early on Monday morning the Minister of Transportation's Daimler disappeared down the drive. 'I rather think he expected to see Mamma,' said Peter. 'I told him what was the matter with her.'

'You shouldn't have done that,' said Paul.

'No, it didn't go down awfully well. He said that he didn't know what things were coming to and that even in the slums such things were not spoken about by children of my age. What a lot he ate! I did my best to make him feel at home, too, by talking about trains.'

'I thought he was a very sensible old man,' said Professor Silenus. 'He was the only person who didn't think it necessary to say something polite about the house. Besides, he told me about a new method of concrete construction they're trying at one of the Government Superannuation Homes.'

Peter and Paul went back to their cylindrical study and began another spelling-lesson.

*

As the last of the guests departed Mrs Beste-Chetwynde reappeared from her little bout of veronal, fresh and exquisite as a seventeenth-century lyric. The meadow of green glass seemed to burst into flower under her feet as she passed from the lift to the cocktail table.

'You poor angels!' she said. 'Did you have the hell of a time with Maltravers? And all those people? I quite forget who asked to come this week-end. I gave up inviting people long ago,' she said, turning to Paul, 'but it didn't make a bit of difference.' She gazed into the opalescent depths of her *absinthe frappé*. 'More and more I feel the need of a husband, but Peter is horribly fastidious.'

'Well, your men are all so awful,' said Peter.

'I sometimes think of marrying old Maltravers,' said Mrs Beste-Chetwynde, 'just to get my own back, only "Margot Maltravers" does sound a little too much, don't you think? And if they give him a peerage, he's bound to choose something quite awful. . . .'

In the whole of Paul's life no one had ever been quite so sweet to him as Margot Beste-Chetwynde was during the next few days. Up and down the shining lift shafts, in and out of the rooms, and along the labyrinthine corridors of the great house he moved in a golden mist. Each morning as he dressed a bird seemed to be singing in his heart, and as he lay down to sleep he would pillow his head against a hand about which still hung a delicate fragrance of Margot Beste-Chetwynde's almost unprocurable scent.

'Paul, dear,' she said one day as hand in hand, after a rather fearful encounter with a swan, they reached the shelter of the lake house, 'I can't bear to think of you going back to that awful school. Do, please, write and tell Dr Fagan that you won't.'

The lake house was an eighteenth-century pavilion, built on a little mound above the water. They stood there for a full minute still hand in hand on the crumbling steps.

'I don't quite see what else I could do,' said Paul.

'Darling, *I* could find you a job.'

'What sort of job, Margot?' Paul's eyes followed the swan gliding serenely across the lake; he did not dare to look at her.

'Well, Paul, you might stay and protect me from swans, mightn't you?' Margot paused and then, releasing her hand, took a cigarette-case from her pocket. Paul struck a match. 'My dear, what an unsteady hand! I'm afraid you're drinking too many of Peter's cocktails. That child has a lot to learn yet about the use of vodka. But seriously I'm sure I can find you a better job. It's absurd your going back to Wales. I still manage a great deal of my father's business, you know, or perhaps you didn't. It was mostly in South America in − in places of entertainment, cabarets and hotels and theatres, you know, and things like that. I'm sure I could find you a job helping in that, if you think you'd like it.'

Paul thought of this gravely. 'Oughtn't I to know Spanish?' he said. It seemed quite a sensible question, but Margot threw away her cigarette with a little laugh and said: 'It's time to go and change. You are being difficult this evening, aren't you?'

Paul thought about this conversation as he lay in his bath − a sunk bath of malachite − and all the time while he dressed and as he tied his tie he trembled from head to foot like one of the wire toys which street vendors dangle from trays.

At dinner Margot talked about matters of daily interest, about some jewels she was having reset, and how they had come back all wrong; and how all the wiring of her London house was being overhauled because of the fear of fire; and how the man she had left in charge of her villa at Cannes had made a fortune at the Casino and given her notice, and she was afraid she might have to go out there to arrange about it; and how the Society for the Preservation of Ancient Buildings was demanding a guarantee that she would not demolish her castle in Ireland; and how her cook seemed to be going off his head that night, the dinner was so dull; and how Bobby Pastmaster was trying to borrow money from her again, on the grounds that she had misled him when she bought his house and that if he had known she was going to pull it down he would have made her pay more. 'Which is not logical of Bobby,' she said. 'The less I valued this house, the less I ought to have paid, surely? Still, I'd better send him something, otherwise he'll go and marry, and I think it may be nice for Peter to have the title when he grows up.'

Later, when they were alone, she said: 'People talk a great deal of nonsense about being rich. Of course it is a bore in some ways, and it means endless work, but I wouldn't be poor, or even moderately well-off, for all the ease in the world. Would you be happy if you were rich, do you think?'

'Well, it depends how I got the money,' said Paul.

'I don't see how that comes in.'

'No, I don't quite mean that. What I mean is that I think there's only one thing that could make me really happy, and if I got that I should be rich too, but it wouldn't matter being rich, you see, because, however rich I was, and I hadn't got what would make me happy, I shouldn't be happy, you see.'

'My precious, that's rather obscure,' said Margot, 'but I think it may mean something rather sweet.' He looked up at her, and her eyes met his unfalteringly. 'If it does, I'm glad,' she added.

'Margot, darling, beloved, please, will you marry me?' Paul was on his knees by her chair, his hands on hers.

'Well, that's rather what I've been wanting to discuss with you all day.' But surely there was a tremor in her voice?

'Does that mean that possibly you might, Margot? Is there a chance that you will?'

'I don't see why not. Of course we must ask Peter about it, and there are other things we ought to discuss first,' and then, quite suddenly, 'Paul, dear, dear creature, come here.'

*

They found Peter in the dining-room eating a peach at the sideboard.

'Hullo, you two!' he said.

'Peter, we've something to tell you,' said Margot. 'Paul says he wants me to marry him.'

'Splendid!' said Peter. 'I *am* glad. Is that what you've been doing in the library?'

'Then you don't mind?' said Paul.

'Mind? It's what I've been trying to arrange all this week. As a matter of fact, that's why I brought you here at all. I think it's altogether admirable,' he said, taking another peach.

'You're the first man he's said that about, Paul. I think it's rather a good omen.'

'Oh, Margot, let's get married at once.'

'My dear, I haven't said that I'm going to yet. I'll tell you in the morning.'

'No, tell me now, Margot. You do like me a little, don't you? Please marry me just terribly soon.'

'I'll tell you in the morning. There're several things I must think about first. Let's go back to the library.'

*

That night Paul found it unusually difficult to sleep. Long after he had shut his book and turned out the light he lay awake, his eyes open, his thoughts racing uncontrollably. As in the first night of his visit, he felt the sleepless, involved genius of the house heavy about his head. He and Margot and Peter and Sir Humphrey Maltravers were just insignificant incidents in the life of the house: this new-born monster to whose birth ageless and forgotten cultures had been in travail. For half an hour he lay looking into the darkness until gradually his thoughts began to separate themselves from himself, and he knew he was falling asleep. Suddenly he was roused to consciousness by the sound of his door opening gently. He could see nothing, but he heard the rustle of silk as someone came into the room. Then the door shut again.

'Paul, are you asleep?'

'Margot!'

'Hush, dear! Don't turn on the light. Where are you?' The silk rustled again as though falling to the ground. 'It's best to make sure, isn't it, darling, before we decide anything? It may be just an idea of yours that you're in love with me. And, you see, Paul, I like you so very much, it would be a pity to make a mistake, wouldn't it?'

But happily there was no mistake, and next day Paul and Margot announced their engagement.

CHAPTER IV

Resurrection

CROSSING the hall one afternoon a few days later, Paul met a short man with a long red beard stumping along behind the footman towards Margot's study.

'Good Lord!' he said.

'Not a word, old boy!' said the bearded man as he passed on.

A few minutes later Paul was joined by Peter. 'I say, Paul,' he said, 'who do you think's talking to Mamma?'

'I know,' said Paul. 'It's a very curious thing.'

'I somehow never felt he was dead,' said Peter. 'I told Clutterbuck that to try and cheer him up.'

'Did it?'

'Not very much,' Peter admitted. 'My argument was that if he'd really gone out to sea he would have left his wooden leg behind with his clothes, but Clutterbuck said he was very sensitive about his leg. I wonder what he's come to see Mamma about?'

A little later they ambushed him in the drive, and Grimes told them. 'Forgive the beaver,' he said, 'but it's rather important at the moment.'

'In the soup again?' asked Paul.

'Well, not exactly, but things have been rather low lately. The police are after me. That suicide didn't go down well. I was afraid it wouldn't. They began to fuss a bit about nobody being found and about my game leg. And then my other wife turned up, and that set them thinking. Hence the vegetation. Clever of you two to spot me.'

They led him back to the house, and Peter mixed him a formidable cocktail, the principal ingredients of which were absinthe and vodka.

'It's the old story,' said Grimes. 'Grimes has fallen on his feet again. By the way, old boy, I have to congratulate you, haven't I? You've done pretty well for yourself, too.' His eye travelled appreciatively over the glass floor, and the pneumatic rubber furniture, and the porcelain ceiling, and the leather-hung walls. 'It's not everyone's taste,' he said, 'but I think you'll be comfortable. Funny thing, I never expected to see you when I came down here.'

'What we want to know,' said Peter, 'is what brought you down to see Mamma at all.'

'Just good fortune,' said Grimes. 'It was like this. After I left Llanabba I was rather at a loose end. I'd borrowed a fiver from Philbrick just before he left, and that got me to London, but for a week or so things were rather thin. I was sitting in a pub one day in Shaftesbury Avenue, feeling my beard rather warm and knowing I only had about five bob left in the world, when I noticed a chap staring at me pretty hard in the other corner of the bar. He came over after a bit and said: "Captain Grimes, I think?" That rather put the wind up me. "No, no, old boy," I said, "quite wrong, rotten shot. Poor old Grimes is dead, drowned. Davy Jones' locker, old boy!" And I made to leave. Of course it wasn't a very sensible thing to say, because, if I hadn't been Grimes, it was a hundred to one against my knowing Grimes was dead, if you see what I mean.

"Pity," he said, "because I heard old Grimes was down on his luck, and I had a job I thought might suit him. Have a drink, anyway." Then I realized who he was. He was an awful stout fellow called Bill, who'd been quartered with me in Ireland. "Bill," I said, "I thought you were a bobby." "That's all right, old boy," said Bill. Well, it appeared that this Bill had gone off to the Argentine after the war and had got taken on as manager of a . . .' – Grimes stopped as though suddenly reminded of something – 'a place of entertainment. Sort of night club, you know. Well, he'd done rather well in that job, and had been put in charge of a whole chain of places of entertainment all along the coast. They're a syndicate owned in England. He'd come back on leave to look for a couple of chaps to go out with him and help. "The Dagos are no use at the job," he said, "not dispassionate enough." Had to be chaps who could control themselves where women were concerned. That's what made him think of me. But it was a pure act of God, our meeting.

'Well, apparently the syndicate was first founded by young Beste-Chetwynde's grandpapa, and Mrs Beste-Chetwynde still takes an interest in it, so I was sent down to interview her and see if she agreed to the appointment. It never occurred to me it was the same Mrs Beste-Chetwynde who came down to the sports the day Prendy got so tight. Only shows how small the world is, doesn't it?'

'Did Mamma give you the job?' asked Peter.

'She did, and fifty pounds advance on my wages, and some jolly sound advice. It's been a good day for Grimes. Heard from the old man lately, by the way?'

'Yes,' said Paul, 'I got a letter this morning,' and he showed it to Grimes:

> *Llanabba Castle,*
> *North Wales.*
>
> My dear Pennyfeather,
>   Thank you for your letter and the enclosed cheque! I need hardly tell you that it is a real disappointment to me to hear that you are not

returning to us next term. I had looked forward to a long and mutually profitable connexion. However my daughters and I join in wishing you every happiness in your married life. I hope you will use your new influence to keep Peter at the school. He is a boy for whom I have great hopes. I look to him as one of my prefects in the future.

The holidays so far have afforded me little rest. My daughters and I have been much worried by the insistence of a young Irish woman of most disagreeable appearance and bearing who claims to be the widow of poor Captain Grimes. She has got hold of some papers which seem to support her claim. The police, too, are continually here asking impertinent questions about the number of suits of clothes my unfortunate son-in-law possessed.

Besides this, I have had a letter from Mr Prendergast stating that he too wishes to resign his post. Apparently he has been reading a series of articles by a popular bishop and has discovered that there is a species of person called a 'Modern Churchman' who draws the full salary of a beneficed clergyman and need not commit himself to any religious belief. This seems to be a comfort to him, but it adds to my own inconvenience.

Indeed, I hardly think that I have the heart to keep on at Llanabba. I have had an offer from a cinema company, the managing director of which, oddly enough, is called Sir Solomon Philbrick, who wish to buy the Castle. They say that its combination of medieval and Georgian architecture is a unique advantage. My daughter Diana is anxious to start a nursing-home or an hotel. So you see that things are not easy.

Yours sincerely,
Augustus Fagan.

There was another surprise in store for Paul that day. Hardly had Grimes left the house when a tall young man with a black hat and thoughtful eyes presented himself at the front door and asked for Mr Pennyfeather. It was Potts.

'My dear fellow,' said Paul, 'I am glad to see you.'

'I saw your engagement in *The Times*,' said Potts, 'and as I was in the neighbourhood, I wondered if you'd let me see the house.'

Paul and Peter led him all over it and explained its intricacies. He admired the luminous ceiling in Mrs Beste-

Chetwynde's study and the indiarubber fungi in the recessed
conservatory and the little drawing-room, of which the floor
was a large kaleidoscope, set in motion by an electric button.
They took him up in the lift to the top of the great pyramidal
tower, from which he could look down on the roofs and domes
of glass and aluminium which glittered like Chanel diamonds
in the afternoon sun. But it was not this that he had come to
see. As soon as he and Paul were alone he said, as though
casually: 'Who was that little man I met coming down the
drive?'

'I think he was something to do with the Society for the
Preservation of Ancient Buildings,' said Paul. 'Why?'

'Are you sure?' asked Potts in evident disappointment. 'How
maddening! I've been on a false scent again.'

'Are you doing Divorce Court shadowings, Potts?'

'No, no, it's all to do with the League of Nations,' said Potts
vaguely, and he called attention to the tank of octopuses which
was so prominent a feature of the room in which they were
standing.

Margot invited Potts to stay to dinner. He tried hard to
make a good impression on Professor Silenus, but in this he
was not successful. In fact, it was probably Potts' visit which
finally drove the Professor from the house. At any rate, he left
early the next morning without troubling to pack or remove
his luggage. Two days later, when they were all out, he arrived
in a car and took away his mathematical instruments, and some
time after that again appeared to fetch two clean handkerchiefs
and a change of underclothes. That was the last time he was
seen at King's Thursday. When Margot and Paul went up to
London they had his luggage packed and left downstairs for
him, in case he should come again, but there it stayed, none
of the male servants finding anything in it that he would care
to wear. Long afterwards Margot saw the head gardener's son
going to church in a *batik* tie of Professor Silenus' period. It
was the last relic of a great genius, for before that King's
Thursday had been again rebuilt.

CHAPTER V
The Latin-American Entertainment Co., Ltd

AT the end of April Peter returned to Llanabba, Dr Fagan
having announced that the sale of the Castle had not been
effected, and Margot and Paul went up to London to make
arrangements for the wedding, which, contrary to all reasonable expectation, Margot decided was to take place in church
with all the barbaric concomitants of bridesmaids, Mendel-
ssohn, and Mumm. But before the wedding she had a good
deal of South American business to see to.

'My first honeymoon was rather a bore,' she said, 'so I'm
not taking any chances with this one. I must get everything
settled before we start, and then we're going to have the three
best months of your life.'

The work seemed to consist chiefly of interviewing young
women for jobs in cabarets and as dancing partners. With some
reluctance Margot allowed Paul to be present one morning as
she saw a new batch. The room in which she conducted her
business was the Sports Room, which had been decorated for
her, in her absence, by little Davy Lennox, the society photographer. Two stuffed buffaloes stood one on each side of the
door. The carpet was of grass-green marked out with white
lines, and the walls were hung with netting. The lights were
in glass footballs, and the furniture was ingeniously designed
of bats and polo-sticks and golf-clubs. Athletic groups of
the early nineties and a painting of a prize ram hung on the
walls.

'It's terribly common,' said Margot, 'but it rather impresses
the young ladies, which is a good thing. Some of them tend
to be rather mannery if they aren't kept in order.'

Paul sat in the corner – on a chair made in the shape of
an inflated Channel swimmer – enraptured at her business
ability. All her vagueness had left her; she sat upright at the
table, which was covered with Balmoral tartan, her pen poised
over an inkpot, which was set in a stuffed grouse, the very

embodiment of the Feminist movement. One by one the girls were shown in.

'Name?' said Margot.

'Pompilia de la Conradine.'

Margot wrote it down.

'Real name?'

'Bessy Brown.'

'Age?'

'Twenty-two.'

'Real age?'

'Twenty-two.'

'Experience?'

'I was at Mrs Rosenbaum's, in Jermyn Street, for two years, mum.'

'Well, Bessy, I'll see what I can do for you. Why did you leave Mrs Rosenbaum's?'

'She said the gentlemen liked a change.'

'I'll just ask her.' Margot took up the telephone, which was held by a boxing-glove. 'Is that Mrs Rosenbaum? This is Latin-American Entertainments, Ltd speaking. Can you tell me about Miss de la Conradine? . . . Oh, that was the reason she left you? Thank you so much! I rather thought that might be it.' She rang off. 'Sorry, Bessy; nothing for you just at present.'

She pressed the bell, which was in the eye of a salmon trout, and another young lady was shown in.

'Name?'

'Jane Grimes.'

'Who sent you to me?'

'The gentleman at Cardiff. He gave me this to give you.' She produced a crumpled envelope and handed it across the table. Margot read the note. 'Yes, I see. So you're new to the business, Jane?'

'Like a babe unborn, mum.'

'But you married?'

'Yes, mum, but it was in the war, and he was very drunk.'

'Where's your husband?'

'Dead, so they do say.'

'That's excellent, Jane. You're just the sort we want. How soon can you sail?'

'How soon would you be wanting me to?'

'Well, there's a vacancy in Rio I'm filling at the end of the week. I'm sending out two very nice girls. Would you like to be going with them?'

'Yes, mum, very pleased, I'm sure.'

'D'you want any money in advance?'

'Well, I could do with a bit to send my dad if you could spare it.'

Margot took some notes from a drawer, counted them, and made out the receipt.

'Sign this, will you? I've got your address. I'll send you your tickets in a day or so. How are you off for clothes?'

'Well, I've got a fine silk dress, but it's at Cardiff with the other things. The gentleman said I'd be getting some new clothes, perhaps.'

'Yes, quite right. I'll make a note of that. The arrangement we generally make is that our agent chooses the clothes and you pay for them out of your salary in instalments.'

Mrs Grimes went out, and another girl took her place.

By luncheon-time Margot Beste-Chetwynde was tired. 'Thank heavens, that's the last of them,' she said. 'Were you terribly bored, my angel?'

'Margot, you're wonderful. You ought to have been an empress.'

'Don't say that you were a Christian slave, dearest.'

'It never occurred to me,' said Paul.

'There's a young man just like your friend Potts on the other side of the street,' said Margot at the window. 'And my dear, he's picked up the last of those poor girls, the one who wanted to take her children and her brother with her.'

'Then it can't be Potts,' said Paul lazily. 'I say, Margot, there was one thing I couldn't understand. Why was it that the less experience those chorus-girls had, the more you seemed to want them? You offered much higher wages to the ones who said they'd never had a job before.'

'Did I, darling? I expect it was because I feel so absurdly happy.'

At the time this seemed quite a reasonable explanation, but, thinking the matter over, Paul had to admit to himself that there had been nothing noticeably light-hearted in Margot's conduct of her business.

'Let's have luncheon out to-day,' said Margot. 'I'm tired of this house.'

They walked across Berkeley Square together in the sunshine. A footman in livery stood on the steps of one of the houses. A hatter's van, emblazoned with the royal arms, trotted past them on Hay Hill, two cockaded figures upright upon the box. A very great lady, bolstered up in an old-fashioned landaulette, bowed to Margot with an inclination she had surely learned in the Court of the Prince Consort. All Mayfair seemed to throb with the heart of Mr Arlen.

Philbrick sat at the next table at the *Maison Basque* eating the bitter little strawberries which are so cheap in Provence and so very expensive in Dover Street.

'Do come and see me some time,' he said. 'I'm living up the street at Batts'.'

'I hear you're buying Llanabba,' said Paul.

'Well, I thought of it,' said Philbrick. 'But I'm afraid it's too far away, really.'

'The police came for you soon after you left,' said Paul.

'They're bound to get me some time,' said Philbrick. 'But thanks for the tip all the same! By the way, you might warn your fiancée that they'll be after her soon, if she's not careful. That League of Nations Committee is getting busy at last.'

'I haven't the least idea what you mean,' said Paul, and returned to his table.

'Obviously the poor man's dotty,' said Margot when he told her of the conversation.

CHAPTER VI
A Hitch in the Wedding Preparations

MEANWHILE half the shops in London were engaged on the wedding preparations. Paul asked Potts to be his best man, but a letter from Geneva declined the invitation. In other circumstances this might have caused him embarrassment, but during the past fortnight Paul had received so many letters and invitations from people he barely remembered meeting that his only difficulty in filling his place was the fear of offending any of his affectionate new friends. Eventually he chose Sir Alastair Digby-Vane-Trumpington, because he felt that, however indirectly, he owed him a great deal of his present good fortune. Sir Alastair readily accepted, at the same time borrowing the money for a new tall hat, his only one having come to grief a few nights earlier.

A letter from Onslow Square, which Paul left unanswered, plainly intimated that Paul's guardian's daughter would take it as a personal slight, and as a severe blow to her social advancement, if she were not chosen as one of the bridesmaids.

For some reason or other, Paul's marriage seemed to inspire the public as being particularly romantic. Perhaps they admired the enterprise and gallantry with which Margot, after ten years of widowhood, voluntarily exposed herself to a repetition of the hundred and one horrors of a fashionable wedding, or perhaps Paul's sudden elevation from schoolmaster to millionaire struck a still vibrant chord of optimism in each of them, so that they said to themselves over their ledgers and typewriters: 'It may be me next time.' Whatever the reason, the wedding was certainly an unparalleled success among the lower orders. Inflamed by the popular Press, a large crowd assembled outside St Margaret's on the eve of the ceremony equipped, as for a first night, with collapsible chairs, sandwiches, and spirit stoves, while by half past two, in spite of heavy rain, it had swollen to such dimensions that the police were forced to make several baton-charges and many guests were crushed almost to death in their attempts to reach the doors, and the route down which Margot had to drive was lined as for a funeral with weeping and hysterical women.

Society was less certain in its approval, and Lady Circumference, for one, sighed for the early nineties, when Edward Prince of Wales, at the head of *ton*, might have given authoritative condemnation to this ostentatious second marriage.

'It's maddenin' Tangent having died just at this time,' she said. 'People may think that that's my reason for refusin'. I can't imagine that *anyone* will go.'

'I hear your nephew Alastair Trumpington is the best man,' said Lady Vanburgh.

'You seem to be as well informed as my chiropodist,' said Lady Circumference with unusual felicity, and all Lowndes Square shook at her departure.

In the unconverted mewses of Mayfair and the upper rooms of Shepherd Market and North Audley Street, where fashionable bachelors lurk disconsolately on their evenings at home, there was open lamentation at the prey that had been allowed to slip through their elegantly gloved fingers, while more than one popular dancing man inquired anxiously at his bank to learn whether his month's remittance had been paid in as usual. But Margot remained loyal to all her old obligations, and invitations to her wedding-reception were accepted by whole bevies of young men who made it their boast that they never went out except to a square meal, while little Davy Lennox, who for three years had never been known to give anyone a 'complimentary sitting', took two eloquent photographs of the back of her head and one of the reflection of her hands in a bowl of ink.

Ten days before the wedding Paul moved into rooms at the Ritz, and Margot devoted herself seriously to shopping. Five or six times a day messengers appeared at his suite bringing little by-products of her activity – now a platinum cigarette-case, now a dressing-gown, now a tie-pin or a pair of links – while Paul, with unaccustomed prodigality, bought two new ties, three pairs of shoes, an umbrella, and a set of Proust.

Margot had fixed his personal allowance at two thousand a year.

Far away in the Adriatic feverish preparations were being made to make Mrs Beste-Chetwynde's villa at Corfu ready for the first weeks of her honeymoon, and the great bed, carved with pineapples, that had once belonged to Napoleon III, was laid out for her reception with fragrant linen and pillows of unexampled softness. All this the newspapers retailed with uncontrolled profusion, and many a young reporter was handsomely commended for the luxuriance of his adjectives.

However, there was a hitch.

Three days before the date fixed for the wedding Paul was sitting in the Ritz opening his morning's post, when Margot rang him up.

'Darling, rather a tiresome thing's happened,' she said. 'You know those girls we sent to Rio the other day? Well, they're stuck at Marseilles, for some reason or other. I can't quite make out why. I think it's something to do with their passports. I've just had a very odd cable from my agent there. He's giving up the job. It's such a bore all this happening just now. I do so want to get everything fixed before Thursday. I wonder if you could be an angel and go over and see to it for me? It's probably only a matter of giving the right man a few hundred francs. If you fly you'll be back in plenty of time. I'd go myself, only you know, don't you, darling, I simply haven't one minute to spare.'

Paul did not have to travel alone. Potts was at Croydon, enveloped in an ulster and carrying in his hand a little attaché case.

'League of Nations business,' he said, and was twice sick during the flight.

At Paris Paul was obliged to charter a special aeroplane. Potts saw him off.

'Why are you going to Marseilles?' he asked. 'I thought you were going to be married.'

'I'm only going there for an hour or two, to see some people on business,' said Paul.

How like Potts, he thought, to suppose that a little journey like this was going to upset his marriage. Paul was beginning to feel cosmopolitan, the Ritz to-day, Marseilles to-morrow, Corfu next day, and afterwards the whole world stood open to him like one great hotel, his way lined for him with bows and orchids. How pathetically insular poor Potts was, he thought, for all his talk of internationalism.

It was late evening when Paul arrived at Marseilles. He dined at Basso's in the covered balcony off bouillabaisse and Meursault at a table from which he could see a thousand lights reflected in the still water. Paul felt very much of a man of the world as he paid his bill, calculated the correct tip, and sat back in the open cab on his way to the old part of the town.

'They'll probably be at *Alice's*, in the Rue de Reynarde,' Margot had said. 'Anyway, you oughtn't to have any difficulty in finding them if you mention my name.'

At the corner of the Rue Ventomargy the carriage stopped. The way was too narrow and too crowded for traffic. Paul paid the driver. '*Merci, Monsieur! Gardez bien votre chapeau,*' he said as he drove off. Wondering what the expression could mean, Paul set off with less certain steps down the cobbled alley. The houses overhung perilously on each side, gaily alight from cellar to garret; between them swung lanterns; a shallow gutter ran down the centre of the path. The scene could scarcely have been more sinister had it been built at Hollywood itself for some orgiastic incident of the Reign of Terror. Such a street in England, Paul reflected, would have been saved long ago by Mr Spire and preserved under a public trust for the sale of brass toasting forks, picture postcards, and 'Devonshire teas'. Here the trade was of a different sort. It did not require very much worldly wisdom to inform him of the character of the quarter he was now in. Had he not, guide-book in hand, traversed the forsaken streets of Pompeii?

No wonder, Paul reflected, that Margot had been so anxious to rescue her protégées from this place of temptation and danger.

A Negro sailor, hideously drunk, addressed Paul in no language known to man, and invited him to have a drink. He hurried on. How typical of Margot that, in all her whirl of luxury, she should still have time to care for the poor girls she had unwittingly exposed to such perils.

Deaf to the polyglot invitations that arose on all sides, Paul pressed on his way. A young lady snatched his hat from his head; he caught a glimpse of her bare leg in a lighted doorway; then she appeared at a window, beckoning him to come in and retrieve it.

All the street seemed to be laughing at him. He hesitated; and then, forsaking, in a moment of panic, both his black hat and his self-possession, he turned and fled for the broad streets and the tram lines where, he knew at heart, was his spiritual home.

*

By daylight the old town had lost most of its terrors. Washing hung out between the houses, the gutters ran with fresh water and the streets were crowded with old women carrying baskets of fish. *Chez Alice* showed no sign of life, and Paul was forced to ring and ring before a tousled old concierge presented himself.

'*Avez-vous les jeunes filles de Madame Beste-Chetwynde?*' Paul asked, acutely conscious of the absurdity of the question.

'Sure, step right along, Mister,' said the concierge; 'she wired us you was coming.'

Mrs Grimes and her two friends were not yet dressed, but they received Paul with enthusiasm in dressing-gowns which might have satisfied the taste for colour of the elder Miss Fagan. They explained the difficulty of the passports, which, Paul thought, was clearly due to some misapprehension by the authorities of their jobs in Rio. They didn't know any French, and of course they had explained things wrong.

He spent an arduous morning at consulates and police bureaux. Things were more difficult than he had thought, and the officials received him either with marked coldness or with incomprehensible winks and innuendo.

Things had been easier six months ago, they said, but now, with the League of Nations – And they shrugged their shoulders despairingly. Perhaps it might be arranged once more, but Madame Beste-Chetwynde must really understand that there were forms that must be respected. Eventually the young ladies were signed on as stewardesses.

'And if they should not go farther with me than Rio,' said the captain, 'well, I have a sufficient staff already. You say there are posts waiting for them there? No doubt their employers will be able to arrange things there with the authorities.'

But it cost Paul several thousand francs to complete the arrangements. 'What an absurd thing the League of Nations seems to be!' said Paul. 'They seem to make it harder to get about instead of easier.' And this, to his surprise, the officials took to be a capital joke.

Paul saw the young ladies to their ship, and all three kissed him good-bye. As he walked back along the quay he met Potts.

'Just arrived by the morning train,' he said. Paul felt strongly inclined to tell him his opinion of the League of Nations, but remembering Potts' prolixity in argument and the urgency of his own departure, he decided to leave his criticisms for another time. He stopped long enough in Marseilles to cable to Margot, 'Everything arranged satisfactorily. Returning this afternoon. All my love,' and then left for Paris by air, feeling that at last he had done something to help.

*

At ten o'clock on his wedding morning Paul returned to the Ritz. It was raining hard, and he felt tired, unshaven and generally woebegone. A number of newspaper reporters were waiting for him outside his suite, but he told them that he could see no one. Inside he found Peter Beste-Chetwynde, incredibly smart in his first morning-coat.

'They've let me come up from Llanabba for the day,' he said. 'To tell you the truth, I'm rather pleased with myself in these clothes. I bought you a buttonhole in case you'd forgotten. I say, Paul, you're looking tired.'

'I am, rather. Turn on the bath for me like an angel.'

When he had had his bath and shaved he felt better. Peter had ordered a bottle of champagne and was a little tipsy. He walked round the room, glass in hand, talking gaily, and every now and then pausing to look at himself in the mirror. 'Pretty smart,' he said, 'particularly the tie; don't you think so, Paul? I think I shall go back to the school like this. That would make them see what a superior person I am. I hope you notice that I gave you the grander buttonhole? I can't tell you what Llanabba is like this term, Paul. Do try and persuade Mamma to take me away. Clutterbuck has left, and Tangent is dead, and the three new masters are quite awful. One is like your friend Potts, only he stutters, and Brolly says he's got a glass eye. He's called Mr Makepeace. Then there's another one with red hair who keeps beating everyone all the time, and the other's rather sweet, really, only he has fits. I don't think the Doctor cares for any of them much. Flossie's been looking rather discouraged all the time. I wonder if Mamma could get her a job in South America? I'm glad you're wearing a waistcoat like that. I nearly did, but I thought perhaps I was a bit young. What do you think? We had a reporter down at the school the other day wanting to know particulars about you. Brolly told a splendid story about how you used to go out swimming in the evenings and swim for hours and hours in the dark composing elegiac verses, and then he spoilt it by saying you had webbed feet and a prehensile tail, which made the chap think he was having his leg pulled. I say, am I terribly in the way?'

As Paul dressed his feelings of well-being began to return. He could not help feeling that he too looked rather smart. Presently Alastair Digby-Vane-Trumpington came in, and drank some champagne.

'This wedding of ours is about the most advertised thing that's happened for a generation,' he said. 'D'you know, the

Sunday Mail has given me fifty pounds to put my name to an article describing my sensations as best man. I'm afraid every one will know it's not me, though; it's too jolly well written. I've had a marvellous letter from Aunt Greta about it, too. Have you seen the presents? The Argentine Chargé d'Affaires has given you the works of Longfellow bound in padded green leather, and the Master of Scone has sent those pewter plates he used to have in his hall.'

Paul fastened the gardenia in his buttonhole, and they went down to luncheon. There were several people in the restaurant obviously dressed for a wedding, and it gave Paul some satisfaction to notice that he was the centre of interest of the whole room. The *maître d'hôtel* offered his graceful good wishes as he led them to their table. Peter, earlier in the morning, had ordered the luncheon.

'I doubt if we shall have time to eat it all,' he said, 'but fortunately the best things all come at the beginning.'

As he was peeling his second gull's egg, Paul was called away to the telephone.

'Darling,' said Margot's voice, 'how are you? I've been so anxious all the time you were away. I had an awful feeling something was going to stop you coming back. Are you all right, dearest? Yes, I'm terribly well. I'm at home having luncheon in my bedroom and feeling, my dear, I can't tell you how virginal, really and truly completely débutante. I hope you'll like my frock. It's Boulanger, darling, do you mind? Good-bye, my sweet. Don't let Peter get too drunk, will you?'

Paul went back to the dining-room.

'I've eaten your eggs,' said Peter. 'I just couldn't help it.'

By two o'clock they had finished their luncheon. Mrs Beste-Chetwynde's second-best Hispano Suiza was waiting in Arlington Street.

'You must just have one more drink with me before we go,' said the best man; 'there's heaps of time.'

'I think perhaps it would be a mistake if I did,' said Peter.

Paul and his best man refilled their glasses with brandy.

'It is a funny thing,' said Alastair Digby-Vane-Trumpington.

'No one could have guessed that when I had the Boller blind in my rooms it was going to end like this.'

Paul turned the liqueur round in his glass, inhaled its rich bouquet for a second, and then held it before him.

'To Fortune,' he said, 'a much-maligned lady!'

*

'Which of you gentlemen is Mr Paul Pennyfeather?'

Paul put down his glass and turned to find an elderly man of military appearance standing beside him.

'I am,' he said. 'But I'm afraid that, if you're from the Press, I really haven't time . . .'

'I'm Inspector Bruce, of Scotland Yard,' said the stranger. 'Will you be so good as to speak to me for a minute outside?'

'Really, officer,' said Paul, 'I'm in a great hurry. I suppose it's about the men to guard the presents. You should have come to me earlier.'

'It's not about presents, and I couldn't have come earlier. The warrant for your arrest has only this minute been issued.'

'Look here,' said Alastair Digby-Vane-Trumpington, 'don't be an ass. You've got the wrong man. They'll laugh at you like blazes over this at Scotland Yard. This is the Mr Pennyfeather who's being married to-day.'

'I don't know anything about that,' said Inspector Bruce. 'All I know is, there's a warrant out for his arrest, and that anything he says may be used as evidence against him. And as for you, young man, I shouldn't attempt to obstruct an officer of the law, not if I was you.'

'It's all some ghastly mistake,' said Paul. 'I suppose I must go with this man. Try and get on to Margot and explain to her.'

Sir Alastair's amiable pink face gaped blank astonishment. 'Good God,' he said, 'how damned funny! At least it would be at any other time.' But Peter, deadly white, had left the restaurant.

END OF PART TWO

PART THREE

CHAPTER I
Stone Walls do not a Prison Make

PAUL'S trial, which took place some weeks later at the Old
Bailey, was a bitter disappointment to the public, the news
editors, and the jury and counsel concerned. The arrest at the
Ritz, the announcement at St Margaret's that the wedding was
postponed, Margot's flight to Corfu, the refusal of bail, the
meals sent in to Paul on covered dishes from Boulestin's, had
been 'front-page stories' every day. After all this, Paul's conviction and sentence were a lame conclusion. At first he
pleaded guilty on all charges, despite the entreaties of his
counsel, but eventually he was galvanized into some show of
defence by the warning of the presiding judge that the law
allowed punishment with the cat-o'-nine tails for offences of
this sort. Even these things were very flat. Potts as chief witness
for the prosecution was unshakeable and was later warmly
commended by the court; no evidence, except of previous
good conduct, was offered by the defence; Margot Beste-
Chetwynde's name was not mentioned, though the judge in
passing sentence remarked that 'no one could be ignorant of
the callous insolence with which, on the very eve of arrest for
this most infamous of crimes, the accused had been preparing
to join his name with one honoured in his country's history,
and to drag down to his own pitiable depths of depravity a
lady of beauty, rank, and stainless reputation. The just censure
of society,' remarked the judge, 'is accorded to those so
inconstant and intemperate that they must take their pleasures
in the unholy market of humanity that still sullies the fame of
our civilization; but for the traders themselves, these human
vampires who prey upon the degradation of their species,

135

society has reserved the right of ruthless suppression.' So Paul was sent off to prison, and the papers headed the column they reserve for home events of minor importance with 'Prison for Ex-Society Bridegroom. Judge on Human Vampires', and there, as far as the public were concerned, the matter ended.

Before this happened, however, a conversation took place which deserves the attention of all interested in the confused series of events of which Paul had become a part. One day, while he was waiting for trial, he was visited in his cell by Peter Beste-Chetwynde.

'Hullo!' he said.

'Hullo, Paul!' said Peter. 'Mamma asked me to come in to see you. She wants to know if you are getting the food all right she's ordered for you. I hope you like it, because I chose most of it myself. I thought you wouldn't want anything very heavy.'

'It's splendid,' said Paul. 'How's Margot?'

'Well, that's rather what I've come to tell you, Paul. Margot's gone away.'

'Where to?'

'She's gone off alone to Corfu. I made her, though she wanted to stay and see your trial. You can imagine what a time we've had with reporters and people. You don't think it awful of her, do you? And listen, there's something else. Can that policeman hear? It's this. You remember that awful old man Maltravers. Well, you've probably seen, he's Home Secretary now. He's been round to see Mamma in the most impossible Oppenheim kind of way, and said that if she'd marry him he could get you out. Of course, he's obviously been reading books. But Mamma thinks it's probably true, and she wants to know how you feel about it. She rather feels the whole thing's rather her fault, really, and, short of going to prison herself, she'll do anything to help. You can't imagine Mamma in prison, can you? Well, would you rather get out now and her marry Maltravers? or wait until you do get out and marry her yourself? She was rather definite about it.'

Paul thought of Professor Silenus' 'In ten years she will be worn out,' but he said:

'I'd rather she waited if you think she possibly can.'

'I thought you'd say that, Paul. I'm so glad. Mamma said: "I won't say I don't know how I shall ever be able to make up to him for all this, because I think he knows I can." Those were her words. I don't suppose you will get more than a year or so, will you?'

'Good Lord, I hope not,' said Paul.

His sentence of seven years' penal servitude was rather a blow. 'In ten years she will be worn out,' he thought as he drove in the prison van to Blackstone Gaol.

*

On his first day there Paul met quite a number of people, some of whom he knew already. The first person was a warder with a low brow and distinctly menacing manner. He wrote Paul's name in the 'Body Receipt Book' with some difficulty and then conducted him to a cell. He had evidently been reading the papers.

'Rather different from the Ritz Hotel, eh?' he said. 'We don't like your kind 'ere, see? And we knows 'ow to treat 'em. You won't find nothing like the Ritz 'ere, you dirty White Slaver.'

But there he was wrong, because the next person Paul met was Philbrick. His prison clothes were ill-fitting, and his chin was unshaven, but he still wore an indefinable air of the grand manner.

'Thought I'd be seeing you soon,' he said. 'They've put me on to reception bath cleaner, me being an old hand. I've been saving the best suit I could find for you. Not a louse on it, hardly.' He threw a little pile of clothes, stamped with the broad arrow, on to the bench.

The warder returned with another, apparently his superior officer. Together they made a careful inventory of all Paul's possessions.

'Shoes, brown, one pair; socks, fancy, one pair; suspenders, black silk, one pair,' read out the warder in a sing-song voice. 'Never saw a bloke with so much clothes.'

There were several checks due to difficulties of spelling, and it was some time before the list was finished.

'Cigarette case, white metal, containing two cigarettes; watch, white metal; tie-pin, fancy' – it had cost Margot considerably more than the warder earned in a year, had he only known – 'studs, bone, one pair; cuff links, fancy, one pair.' The officers looked doubtfully at Paul's gold cigar piercer, the gift of the best man. 'What's this 'ere?'

'It's for cigars,' said Paul.

'Not so much lip!' said the warder, banging him on the top of his head with the pair of shoes he happened to be holding. 'Put it down as "instrument". That's the lot,' he said, 'unless you've got false teeth. You're allowed to keep them, only we must make a note of it.'

'No,' said Paul.

'Truss or other surgical appliance?'

'No,' said Paul.

'All right! You can go to the bath.'

Paul sat for the regulation ten minutes in the regulation nine inches of warm water – which smelt reassuringly of disinfectant – and then put on his prison clothes. The loss of his personal possessions gave him a curiously agreeable sense of irresponsibility.

'You look a treat,' said Philbrick.

Next he saw the Medical Officer, who sat at a table covered with official forms.

'Name?' said the Doctor.

'Pennyfeather.'

'Have you at any time been detained in a mental home or similar institution? If so, give particulars.'

'I was at Scone College, Oxford, for two years,' said Paul.

The Doctor looked up for the first time. 'Don't you dare to make jokes here, my man,' he said, 'or I'll soon have you in the strait-jacket in less than no time.'

'Sorry,' said Paul.

'Don't speak to the Medical Officer unless to answer a question,' said the warder at his elbow.

'Sorry,' said Paul, unconsciously, and was banged on the head.

'Suffering from consumption or any contagious disease?' asked the M.D.

'Not that I know of,' said Paul.

'That's all,' said the Doctor. 'I have certified you as capable of undergoing the usual descriptions of punishment as specified below, to wit, restraint of handcuffs, leg-chains, cross-irons, body-belt, canvas dress, close confinement, No. 1 diet, No. 2 diet, birch-rod, and cat-o'-nine-tails. Any complaint?'

'But must I have all these at once?' asked Paul, rather dismayed.

'You will if you ask impertinent questions. Look after that man, officer; he's obviously a troublesome character.'

'Come 'ere, you,' said the warder. They went up a passage and down two flights of iron steps. Long galleries with iron railings stretched out in each direction, giving access to innumerable doors. Wire-netting was stretched between the landings. 'So don't you try no monkey-tricks. Suicide isn't allowed in this prison. See?' said the warder. 'This is your cell. Keep it clean, or you'll know the reason why, and this is your number.' He buttoned a yellow badge on to Paul's coat.

'Like a flag-day,' said Paul.

'Shut up, you — —,' remarked the warder, and locked the door.

'I suppose I shall learn to respect these people in time,' thought Paul. 'They all seem so much less awe-inspiring than anyone I ever met.'

His next visit was from the Schoolmaster. The door was unlocked, and a seedy-looking young man in a tweed suit came into the cell.

'Can you read and write, D.4.12?' asked the newcomer.

'Yes,' said Paul.

'Public or secondary education?'

'Public,' said Paul. His school had been rather sensitive on this subject.

'What was your standard when you left school?'

'Well, I don't quite know. I don't think we had standards.'

The Schoolmaster marked him down as 'Memory defective' on a form and went out. Presently he returned with a book.

'You must do your best with that for the next four weeks,' he said. 'I'll try and get you into one of the morning classes. You won't find it difficult, if you can read fairly easily. You see, it begins there,' he said helpfully, showing Paul the first page.

It was an English Grammar published in 1872.

'*A syllable is a single sound made by one simple effort of the voice,*' Paul read.

'Thank you,' he said; 'I'm sure I shall find it useful.'

'You can change it after four weeks if you can't get on with it,' said the Schoolmaster. 'But I should stick to it, if you can.'

Again the door was locked.

Next came the Chaplain. 'Here is your Bible and a book of devotion. The Bible stays in the cell always. You can change the book of devotion any week if you wish to. Are you Church of England? Services are voluntary – that is to say, you must either attend all or none.' The Chaplain spoke in a nervous and hurried manner. He was new to his job, and he had already visited fifty prisoners that day, one of whom had delayed him for a long time with descriptions of a vision he had seen the night before.

'Hullo, Prendy!' said Paul.

Mr Prendergast looked at him nervously. 'I didn't recognize you,' he said. 'People look so much alike in those clothes. This is most disturbing, Pennyfeather. As soon as I saw you'd been convicted I was afraid they might send you here. Oh dear! oh dear! It makes everything still more difficult!'

'What's the matter, Prendy? Doubts again?'

'No, no, discipline, my old trouble. I've only been at the job a week. I was very lucky to get it. My bishop said he thought there was more opening for a Modern Churchman in this kind of work than in the parishes. The Governor is very modern too. But criminals are just as bad as boys, I find. They pretend to make confessions and tell me the most dreadful things just to see what I'll say, and in chapel they laugh so much that the warders spend all their time correcting them. It makes the services seem so irreverent. Several of them got put on No. 1 diet this morning for singing the wrong words to one of the hymns, and of course that only makes me more unpopular. Please, Pennyfeather, if you don't mind, you mustn't call me Prendy, and if anyone passes the cell will you stand up when you're talking to me. You're supposed to, you see, and the Chief Warder has said some very severe things to me about maintaining discipline.'

At this moment the face of the warder appeared at the peephole in the door.

'I trust you realize the enormity of your offence and the justice of your punishment?' said Mr Prendergast in a loud voice. 'Pray for penitence.'

A warder came into the cell.

'Sorry to disturb you, sir, but I've got to take this one to see the Governor. There's D.4.18 down the way been asking for you for days. I said I'd tell you, only, if you'll forgive my saying so, I shouldn't be too soft with 'im, sir. We know 'im of old. 'E's a sly old devil, begging your pardon, sir, and 'e's only religious when 'e thinks it'll pay.'

'I think that I am the person to decide that, officer,' said Mr Prendergast with some dignity. 'You may take D.4.12 to the Governor.'

Sir Wilfred Lucas-Dockery had not been intended by nature or education for the Governor of a prison; his appointment was the idea of a Labour Home Secretary who had been impressed by an appendix on the theory of penology which he had contributed to a report on the treatment of 'Conscientious Objectors'. Up to that time Sir Wilfred had held the Chair of Sociology at a Midland university; only his intimate friends and a few specially favoured pupils knew that behind his mild and professional exterior he concealed an ardent ambition to serve in the public life of his generation. He stood twice for Parliament, but so diffidently that his candidature passed almost unnoticed. Colonel MacAdder, his predecessor in office, a veteran of numberless unrecorded campaigns on the Afghan frontier, had said to him on his retirement: 'Good luck, Sir Wilfred! If I may give you a piece of advice, it's this. Don't bother about the lower warders or the prisoners. Give hell to the man immediately below you, and you can rely on him to pass it on with interest. If you make a prison bad enough, people'll take jolly good care to keep out of it. That's been my policy all through, and I'm proud of it' (a policy which soon became quite famous in the society of Cheltenham Spa).

Sir Wilfred, however, had his own ideas. 'You must understand,' he said to Paul, 'that it is my aim to establish personal contact with each of the men under my care. I want you to take a pride in your prison and in your work here. So far as possible, I like the prisoners to carry on with their avocations in civilized life. What's this man's profession, officer?'

'White Slave traffic, sir.'

'Ah yes. Well, I'm afraid you won't have much opportunity for that here. What else have you done?'

'I was nearly a clergyman once,' said Paul.

'Indeed? Well, I hope in time, if I find enough men with the same intention, to get together a theological class. You've no doubt met the Chaplain, a very broad-minded man. Still for the present we are only at the beginning. The Government regulations are rather uncompromising. For the first four weeks you will have to observe the solitary confinement ordained by law. After that we will find you something more creative. We don't want you to feel that your personality is being stamped out. Have you any experience of art leather work?'

'No, sir.'

'Well, I might put you into the Arts and Crafts Workshop. I came to the conclusion many years ago that almost all crime is due to the repressed desire for aesthetic expression. At last we have the opportunity for testing it. Are you an extrovert or an introvert?'

'I'm afraid I'm not sure, sir.'

'So few people are. I'm trying to induce the Home Office to install an official psycho-analyst. Do you read the *New Nation*,

I wonder? There is rather a flattering article this week about
our prison called *The Lucas-Dockery Experiments*. I like the prisoners to know these things. It gives them corporate pride. I may
give you one small example of the work we are doing that
affects your own case. Up till now all offences connected with
prostitution have been put into the sexual category. Now I
hold that an offence of your kind is essentially acquisitive and
shall grade it accordingly. It does not, of course, make any
difference as far as your conditions of imprisonment are concerned – the routine of penal servitude is prescribed by Standing Orders – but you see what a difference it makes to the
annual statistics.'

'The human touch,' said Sir Wilfred after Paul had been
led from the room. 'I'm sure it makes all the difference. You
could see with that unfortunate man just now what a difference
it made to him to think that, far from being a mere nameless
slave, he has now become part of a great revolution in
statistics.'

'Yes, sir,' said the Chief Warder, 'and, by the way, there
are two more attempted suicides being brought up to-morrow.
You must really be more strict with them, sir. Those sharp
tools you've issued to the Arts and Crafts School is just putting
temptation in the men's way.'

*

Paul was once more locked in, and for the first time had the
opportunity of examining his cell. There was little to interest
him. Besides his Bible, his book of devotion – *Prayers on Various
Occasions of Illness, Uncertainty, and Loss, by the Rev. Septimus Bead,
M.A., Edinburgh*, 1863 – and his English Grammar, there was
a little glazed pint pot, a knife and spoon, a slate and slate-
pencil, a salt-jar, a metal water-can, two earthenware vessels,
some cleaning materials, a plank bed upright against the wall,
a roll of bedding, a stool, and a table. A printed notice
informed him that he was not to look out of the window. Three
printed cards on the wall contained a list of other punishable

offences, which seemed to include every human activity, some Church of England prayers, and an explanation of the 'system of progressive stages'. There was also a typewritten 'Thought for the Day', one of Sir Wilfred Lucas-Dockery's little innovations. The message for the first day of Paul's imprisonment was: '*SENSE OF SIN IS SENSE OF WASTE, the Editor of the "Sunday Express*" '. Paul studied the system of progressive stages with interest. After four weeks, he read, he would be allowed to join in associated labour, to take half an hour's exercise on Sundays, to wear a stripe on his arm, if illiterate to have school instruction, to take one work of fiction from the library weekly, and, if special application were made to the Governor, to exhibit four photographs of his relatives or of approved friends; after eight weeks, provided that his conduct was perfectly satisfactory, he might receive a visit of twenty minutes' duration and write and receive a letter. Six weeks later he might receive another visit and another letter and another library book weekly.

Would Davy Lennox's picture of the back of Margot's head be accepted as the photograph of an approved friend, he wondered?

After a time his door was unlocked again and opened a few inches. A hand thrust in a tin, and a voice said, 'Pint pot quick!' Paul's mug was filled with cocoa, and the door was again locked. The tin contained bread, bacon, and beans. That was the last interruption for fourteen hours. Paul fell into a reverie. It was the first time he had been really alone for months. How very refreshing it was, he reflected.

*

The next four weeks of solitary confinement were among the happiest of Paul's life. The physical comforts were certainly meagre, but at the Ritz Paul had learned to appreciate the inadequacy of purely physical comfort. It was so exhilarating, he found, never to have to make any decision on any subject, to be wholly relieved from the smallest consideration of time, meals, or clothes, to have no anxiety ever about what kind of impression he was making; in fact, to be free. At some rather chilly time in the early morning a bell would ring, and the warder would say, 'Slops outside!'; he would rise, roll up his bedding, and dress; there was no need to shave, no hesitation about what tie he should wear, none of the fidgeting with studs and collars and links that so distracts the waking moments of civilized man. He felt like the happy people in the advertisements for shaving soap who seem to have achieved very simply that peace of mind so distant and so desirable in the early morning. For about an hour he stitched away at a mail-bag, until his door was again unlocked to admit a hand with a lump of bread and a large ladle of porridge. After breakfast he gave a cursory polish to the furniture and crockery of his cell and did some more sewing until the bell rang for chapel. For a quarter of an hour or twenty minutes he heard Mr Prendergast blaspheming against the beauties of sixteenth-century diction. This was certainly a bore, and so was the next hour during which he had to march round the prison square, where between concentric paths of worn asphalt a few melancholy cabbages showed their heads. Some of the men during this period used to fall out under the pretence of tying a shoe-lace and take furtive bites at the leaves of the vegetables. If observed they were severely punished. Paul never felt any temptation to do this. After that the day was unbroken save for luncheon, supper, and the Governor's inspection. The heap of sacking which every day he was to turn into mail-bags was supposed by law to keep him busy for nine hours. The prisoners in the cells on either side of him, who were not quite in their right minds, the warder told Paul, found some difficulty in finishing their task before lights out. Paul found that with the least exertion he had finished long before supper, and spent the evenings in meditation and in writing up on his slate the thoughts which had occurred to him during the day.

CHAPTER II
The Lucas-Dockery Experiments

SIR WILFRED LUCAS-DOCKERY, as has already been suggested, combined ambition, scholarship, and genuine optimism in a degree rarely found in his office. He looked forward to a time when the Lucas-Dockery experiments should be recognized as the beginning of a new epoch in penology, and he rehearsed in his mind sentences from the social histories of the future which would contain such verdicts as '*One of the few important events of this Labour Government's brief tenure of power was the appointment as Governor of Blackstone Gaol of Sir Wilfred Lucas-Dockery. The administration of this intrepid and far-seeing official is justly regarded as the foundation of the present system of criminal treatment. In fact, it may safely be said that no single man occupies so high a place in the history of the social reform of his century, etc.*' His eminent qualities, however, did not keep him from many severe differences of opinion with the Chief Warder. He was sitting in his study one day working at a memorandum for the Prison Commissioners – one of the neglected series of memoranda whose publication after his retirement indicated Sir Wilfred's claim to be the pioneer of artificial sunlight in prisons – when the Chief Warder interrupted him.

'A bad report from the Bookbinding Shop, sir. The instructor says that a practice is growing among the men of eating the paste issued to them for their work. They say it is preferable to their porridge. We shall either have to put on another warder to supervise the bookbinding or introduce something into the paste which will make it unpalatable.'

'Has the paste any nutritive value?' asked Sir Wilfred.

'I couldn't say, sir.'

'Weigh the men in the Bookbinding Shop, and then report to me any increase in weight. How many times must I ask you to ascertain *all* the facts before reporting on any case?'

'Very good, sir! And there's a petition from D.4.12. He's finished his four weeks' solitary, and he wants to know if he can keep at it for another four.'

'I disapprove of cellular labour. It makes a man introvert. Who is D.4.12?'

'Long sentence, sir, waiting transference to Egdon.'

'I'll see D.4.12 myself.'

'Very good, sir!'

Paul was led in.

'I understand you wish to continue cellular labour instead of availing yourself of the privilege of working in association. Why is that?'

'I find it so much more interesting, sir,' said Paul.

'It's a most irregular suggestion,' said the Chief Warder. 'Privileges can only be forfeited by a breach of the regulations witnessed and attested by two officers. Standing Orders are most emphatic on the subject.'

'I wonder whether you have narcissistic tendencies?' said the Governor. 'The Home Office has not as yet come to any decision about my application for a staff psycho-analyst.'

'Put him in the observation cell,' said the Chief Warder. 'That brings out any insanity. I've known several cases of men you could hardly have told were mad – just eccentric, you know – who've been put on observation, and after a few days they've been raving lunatics. Colonel MacAdder was a great believer in the observation cells.'

'Did you lead a very lonely life before conviction? Perhaps you were a shepherd or a lighthouse-keeper, or something of the kind?'

'No, sir.'

'Most curious. Well, I will consider your case and give you my answer later.'

Paul was led back to his cell, and next day was again summoned before the Governor.

'I have considered your application,' said Sir Wilfred, 'with the most minute care. In fact, I have decided to include it in

my forthcoming work on the criminal mind. Perhaps you would
like to hear what I have written about you?'

Case R., he read:

*A young man of respectable family and some education. No previous
criminal record. Committed to seven years' penal servitude for traffic in
prostitution. Upon completing his first four weeks R. petitioned for
extension of cellular labour. Treatment as prescribed by Standing Orders:
either* (a) *detention in observation cell for the Medical Officer to satisfy
himself about the state of the prisoner's mind, or* (b) *compulsory
work in association with other prisoners unless privilege forfeited by
misdemeanour.*

*Treatment by Sir Wilfred Lucas-Dockery. – I decided that R. was
suffering from misanthropic tendencies induced by a sense of his own
inferiority in the presence of others. R.'s crime was the result of an attempt
to assert individuality at the expense of community. (Cf. Cases D, G,
and I.) Accordingly I attempted to break down his social inhibitions by
a series of progressive steps. In the first stage he exercised for half an
hour in the company of one other prisoner. Conversation was allowed
during this period upon approved topics, history, philosophy, public events,
etc., the prisoners being chosen among those whose crimes would tend as
little as possible to aggravate and encourage R.'s.*

'I have not yet thought out the other stages of your treatment,' said Sir Wilfred, 'but you can see that individual
attention is being paid to your reclamation. It may cause you
some gratification to realize that, thanks to my report, you may
in time become a case of scientific interest throughout the
world. Sir Wilfred Lucas- Dockery's treatment of Case R. may
haply become a precedent for generations yet unborn. That is
something to lift you above the soul-destroying monotony of
routine, is it not?'

Paul was led away.

'The men in the kitchen have lodged a complaint that they
cannot work with C.2.9,' said the Chief Warder. 'They say he
has an infectious skin disease all over his hands.'

'I can't be worried with things like that,' said the Governor
irritably. 'I am trying to decide upon Case R.'s – I mean
D.4.12's – third stage of reclamation.'

*

Case R. of the Lucas-Dockery experiments began on the new *régime* that afternoon.

'Come out,' said the warder, unlocking his cell, 'and bring your 'at.'

The parade ground, empty of its revolving squads, looked particularly desolate.

'Stand there and don't move till I come back,' said the warder.

Presently he returned with a little bony figure in prison dress.

'This 'ere's your pal,' he said, 'this 'ere's the path you've got to walk on. Neither of you is to touch the other or any part of 'is clothing. Nothing is to be passed from one to the other. You are to keep at a distance of one yard and talk of 'istory, philosophy, or kindred subjects. When I rings the bell you stops talking, see? Your pace is to be neither quicker nor slower than average walking-pace. Them's the Governor's instructions, and Gawd 'elp yer if yer does anything wrong. Now walk.'

'This is a silly dodge,' said the little man. 'I've been in six prisons, and I never seen nothing to touch it. Most irregular. You doesn't know where you are these days. This blinking prison is going to the dogs. Look at the Chaplain. Wears a wig!'

'Are you here for long?' asked Paul politely.

'Not this time. They couldn't get a proper charge against me. "Six months for loitering with intent." They'd been watching me for weeks, but I wasn't going to let them have a chance this time. Now six months is a very decent little sentence, if you take my meaning. One picks up with old friends, and you like it all the more when you comes out. I never minds six months. What's more, I'm known here, so I always gets made "landing cleaner". I expect you've seen me hand often enough coming round with the grub. The warders know me, see, so they always keeps the job open for me if they hears I'm coming back. If you're nice to 'em the first two or three times you're 'ere, they'll probably do the same for you.'

'Is it a very good job?'

'Well, not as jobs go, but it's a nice start. The best job of all is Reception-cleaner. One doesn't get that for years, unless you've special recommendations. You see, you has all the people coming in fresh from outside, and you hears all the news and gets tobacco sometimes and racing tips. Did you see the cleaner when you came in? Know who he is?'

'Yes,' said Paul, 'as a matter of fact, I do. He's called Philbrick.'

'No, no, old man, you've got the wrong chap. I mean a big stout man. Talks a lot about hotels and restaurants.'

'Yes, that's the man I mean.'

'Why, don't you know who that is? That's the Governor's brother: Sir Solomon Lucas-Dockery. Told me so hisself. 'Ere for arson. Burnt a castle in Wales. You can see he's a toff.'

CHAPTER III
The Death of a Modern Churchman

SOME days later Paul entered on another phase of his recla-mation. When he came into the prison-square for his afternoon exercise he found that his companion's place had been taken by a burly man of formidable aspect. He had red hair and beard, and red-rimmed eyes, and vast red hands which twirled convulsively at his sides. He turned his ox-like eyes on Paul and gave a slight snarl of welcome.

'Your new pal,' said the warder. 'Get on with it.'

'How do you do?' said Paul politely. 'Are you here for long?'

'Life,' said the other. 'But it doesn't matter much. I look daily for the Second Coming.'

They marched on in silence.

'Do you think that this a good plan of the Governor's?' asked Paul.

'Yes,' said his companion. They walked on in silence, once round, twice round, three times round.

'Talk, you two,' shouted the warder. 'That's your instructions. Talk.'

'It makes a change,' said the big man.

'What are you here for?' asked Paul. 'You don't mind my asking, do you?'

'It's all in the Bible,' said the big man. 'You should read about it there. Figuratively, you know,' he added. 'It wouldn't be plain to you, I don't suppose, not like it is to me.'

'It's not an easy book to understand, is it?'

'It's not understanding that's needed. It's vision. Do you ever have visions?'

'No, I'm afraid I don't.'

'Nor does the Chaplain. He's no Christian. It was a vision brought me here, an angel clothed in flame, with a crown of flame on his head, crying "Kill and spare not. The Kingdom is at hand." Would you like to hear about it? I'll tell you. I'm a carpenter by profession, or at least I was, you understand.' He spoke with a curious blend of cockney and Biblical English. 'Not a joiner – a cabinet-maker. Well, one day I was just sweeping out the shop before shutting up when the angel of the Lord came in. I didn't know who it was at first. "Just in time," I said. "What can I do for you?" Then I noticed that all about him there was a red flame and a circle of flame over his head, same as I've been telling you. Then he told me how the Lord had numbered His elect and the day of tribulation was at hand. "Kill and spare not," he says. I'd not been sleeping well for some time before this. I'd been worrying about my soul and whether I was saved. Well, all that night I thought of what the angel had told me. I didn't see his meaning, not at first, same as you wouldn't. Then it all came to me in a flash. Unworthy that I am, I am the Lord's appointed,' said the carpenter. 'I am the sword of Israel; I am the lion of the Lord's elect.'

'And did you kill anybody?' asked Paul.

'Unworthy that I am, I smote the Philistine; in the name of the Lord of hosts, I struck off his head. It was for a sign of

Israel. And now I am gone into captivity, and the mirth is turned into weeping, but the Lord shall deliver me in His appointed time. Woe unto the Philistine in that day! woe unto the uncircumcised! It were better that a stone were hanged about his neck and he were cast into the depths of the sea.'

The warder rang his bell. 'Inside, you two!' he shouted.

'Any complaints?' asked the Governor on his rounds.

'Yes, sir,' said Paul.

The Governor looked at him intently. 'Are you the man I put under special treatment?'

'Yes, sir.'

'Then it's ridiculous to complain. What is it?'

'I have reason to believe that the man I have to take exercise with is a dangerous lunatic.'

'Complaints by one prisoner about another can only be considered when substantiated by the evidence of a warder or of two other prisoners,' said the Chief Warder.

'Quite right,' said the Governor. 'I never heard a more ridiculous complaint. All crime is a form of insanity. I myself chose the prisoner with whom you exercise. I chose him for his peculiar suitability. Let me hear no more on this subject, please.'

That afternoon Paul spent another disquieting half-hour on the square.

'I've had another vision,' said the mystical homicide. 'But I don't yet know quite what it portends. No doubt I shall be told.'

'Was it a very beautiful vision?' asked Paul.

'No words can describe the splendour of it. It was all crimson and wet like blood. I saw the whole prison as if it were carved of ruby, hard and glittering, and the warders and the prisoners creeping in and out like little red ladybirds. And then as I watched all the ruby became soft and wet, like a great sponge soaked in wine, and it was dripping and melting into a great lake of scarlet. Then I woke up. I don't know the meaning of it yet, but I feel that the hand of the Lord is hanging over this prison. D'you ever feel like that, as though it were built in the jaws of a beast? I sometimes dream of a great red tunnel like the throat of a beast and men running down it, sometimes one by one and sometimes in great crowds, running down the throat of the beast, and the breath of the beast is like the blast of a furnace. D'you ever feel like that?'

'I'm afraid not,' said Paul. 'Have they given you an interesting library book?'

'*Lady Almina's Secret*,' said the lion of the Lord's elect. 'Pretty soft stuff, old-fashioned, too. But I keep reading the Bible. There's a lot of killing in that.'

'Dear me, you seem to think about killing a great deal.'

'I do. It's my mission, you see,' said the big man simply.

*

Sir Wilfred Lucas-Dockery felt very much like Solomon at ten o'clock every morning of the week except Sunday. It was then that he sat in judgement upon the cases of misconduct among the prisoners that were brought to his notice. From his chair Colonel MacAdder had delivered sentence in undeviating accordance with the spirit and the letter of the Standing Orders Concerning the Government of Her Majesty's Prisons, dispensing automatic justice like a slot machine: in went the offence; out came the punishment. Not so Wilfred Lucas-Dockery. Never, he felt, was his mind more alert or resourceful or his vast accumulation of knowledge more available than at his little court of summary justice. 'No one knows what to expect,' complained warders and prisoners alike.

'Justice,' said Sir Wilfred, 'is the capacity for regarding each case as an entirely new problem.' After a few months of his administration, Sir Wilfred was able to point with some pride to a marked diminution in the number of cases brought before him.

One morning, soon after Paul began on his special *régime* of reclamation, his companion was called up before the Governor.

'God bless my soul!' said Sir Wilfred; 'that's the man I put on special treatment. What is he here for?'

'I was on night duty last night between the hours of 8 p.m. and 4 a.m.,' testified the warder in a sing-song voice, 'when my attention was attracted by sounds of agitation coming from the prisoner's cell. Upon going to the observation hole I observed the prisoner pacing up and down his cell in a state of high excitement. In one hand he held his Bible, and in the other a piece of wood which he had broken from his stool. His eyes were staring; he was breathing heavily, and at times muttering verses of the Bible. I remonstrated with the prisoner when he addressed me in terms prejudicial to good discipline.'

'What are the words complained of?' asked the Chief Warder.

'He called me a Moabite, an abomination of Moab, a wash-pot, an unclean thing, an uncircumcised Moabite, an idolater, and a whore of Babylon, sir.'

'I see. What do you advise, officer?'

'A clear case of insubordination, sir,' said the Chief Warder. 'Try him on No. 1 diet for a bit.'

But when he asked the Chief Warder's opinion, Sir Wilfred was not really seeking advice. He liked to emphasize in his own mind, and perhaps that of the prisoner, the difference between the official view and his own.

'What would you say was the most significant part of the evidence?' he asked.

The Chief Warder considered. 'I think whore of Babylon, on the whole, sir.'

Sir Wilfred smiled as a conjurer may who has forced the right card.

'Now I,' he said, 'am of different opinion. It may surprise you, but I should say that the *significant* thing about this case was the fact that the prisoner held a piece of the stool.'

'Destruction of prison property,' said the Chief Warder. 'Yes, that's pretty bad.'

'Now what was your profession before conviction?' asked the Governor, turning to the prisoner.

'Carpenter, sir.'

'*I knew it,*' said the Governor triumphantly. 'We have another case of the frustrated creative urge. Now listen, my man. It is very wrong of you to insult the officer, who is clearly none of the things you mentioned. He symbolizes the just disapproval of society and is, like all the prison staff, a member of the Church of England. But I understand your difficulty. You have been used to creative craftsmanship, have you not, and you find prison life deprives you of the means of self-expression, and your energies find vent in these foolish outbursts? I will see to it that a bench and a set of carpenter's tools are provided for you. The first thing you shall do is to mend the piece of furniture you so wantonly destroyed. After that we will find other work for you in your old trade. You may go. Get to the cause of the trouble,' Sir Wilfred added when the prisoner was led away; 'your Standing Orders may repress the symptoms; they do not probe to the underlying cause.'

*

Two days later the prison was in a state of intense excitement. Something had happened. Paul woke as the bell rang at the usual time, but it was nearly half an hour before the doors were unlocked. He heard the warder's 'Slops outside!' getting nearer and nearer, interjected with an occasional 'Don't ask questions,' 'Mind your own business,' or a sinister 'You'll know soon enough,' in reply to the prisoners' questions. They, too, had sensed something unusual. Perhaps it was an outbreak of some disease – spotted fever, Paul thought, or a national disaster in the world outside – a war or revolution. In their enforced silence the nerves of all the men were tightened to an acuteness of perception. Paul read wholesale massacres in the warder's face.

'Anything wrong?' he asked.

'I should bleeding well say there was,' said the warder, 'and the next man as asks me a question is going to cop it hot.'

Paul began scrubbing out his cell. Dissatisfied curiosity contended in his thoughts with irritation at this interruption of routine. Two warders passed his door talking.

'I don't say I'm not sorry for the poor bird. All I says is, it was time the Governor had a lesson.'

'It might have been one of us,' said the other warder in a hushed voice.

Breakfast arrived. As the hand appeared at his door Paul whispered: 'What's happened?'

'Why, ain't you 'eard? There's been a murder, shocking bloodthirsty.'

'Get on there,' roared the warder in charge of the landing.

So the Governor had been murdered, thought Paul; he had been a mischievous old bore. Still, it was very disturbing, for the news of a murder which was barely noticed in the gay world of trams and tubes and boxing-matches caused an electric terror in this community of silent men. The interval between breakfast and chapel seemed interminable. At last the bell went. The doors were opened again. They marched in silence to the chapel. As it happened, Philbrick was in the next seat to Paul. The warders sat on raised seats, watchful for any attempt at conversation. The hymn was the recognized time for the exchange of gossip. Paul waited for it impatiently. Clearly it was not the Governor who had been murdered. He stood on the chancel steps, Prayer-Book in hand. Mr Prendergast was nowhere to be seen. The Governor conducted the service. The Medical Officer read the lessons, stumbling heavily over the longer words. Where was Mr Prendergast?

At last the hymn was announced. The organ struck up, played with great feeling by a prisoner who until his conviction had been assistant organist at a Welsh cathedral. All over the chapel the men filled their chests for a burst of conversation.

> 'O God, our help in ages past,' sang Paul.
>   'Where's Prendergast to-day?'
> 'What, ain't you 'eard? 'e's been done in.'
>   'And our eternal home.'

> 'Old Prendy went to see a chap
>   What said he'd seen a ghost;

Well, he was dippy, and he'd got
    A mallet and a saw.'

'Who let the madman have the things?'
    'The Governor; who d'you think?
He asked to be a carpenter,
    He sawed off Prendy's head.

'A pal of mine what lives next door,
    'E 'eard it 'appening;
The warder must 'ave 'eard it too,
    'E didn't interfere.'

'Time, like an ever-rolling stream,
    Bears all its sons away.'
'Poor Prendy 'ollered fit to kill
    For nearly 'alf an hour.

'Damned lucky it was Prendergast,
    Might 'ave been you or me!
The warder says – and I agree –
    It serves the Governor right.'

                                        'Amen.'

From all points of view it was lucky that the madman had chosen Mr Prendergast for attack. Some people even suggested that the choice had been made in a more responsible quarter. The death of a prisoner or warder would have called for a Home Office inquiry which might seriously have discouraged the Lucas-Dockery reforms and also reflected some discredit upon the administration of the Chief Warder. Mr Prendergast's death passed almost unnoticed. His assassin was removed to Broadmoor, and the life of the prison went on smoothly. It was observed, however, that the Chief Warder seemed to have more influence with his superior than he had had before. Sir Wilfred concentrated his attention upon the statistics, and the life of the prison was equitably conducted under the Standing

Orders. It was quite like it had been in old MacAdder's day, the warders observed. But Paul did not reap the benefits of this happy reversion to tradition, because some few days later he was removed with a band of others to the Convict Settlement at Egdon Heath.

CHAPTER IV
Nor Iron Bars a Cage

THE granite walls of Egdon Heath Penal Settlement are visible, when there is no mist, from the main road, and it is not uncommon for cars to stop there a few moments while the occupants stand up and stare happily about them. They are looking for convicts, and as often as not they are rewarded by seeing move across the heath before them a black group of men chained together and uniformly dressed, with a mounted and armed warder riding at their side. They give an appearance of industry which on investigation is quite illusionary, for so much of the day at Egdon is taken up with marching to and from the quarries, in issuing and counting tools, in guarding and chaining and releasing the workmen, that there is very little work done. But there is usually something to be seen from the road, enough, anyway, to be imagined from the very aspect of the building to send the trippers off to their teas with their consciences agreeably unquiet at the memory of small dishonesties in railway trains, inaccurate income tax returns, and the hundred and one minor infractions of law that are inevitable in civilized life.

Paul arrived from Blackstone late one afternoon in early autumn with two warders and six other long-sentence prisoners. The journey had been spent in an ordinary third-class railway carriage, where the two warders smoked black tobacco in cheap little wooden pipes and were inclined towards conversation.

'You'll find a lot of improvements since you were here last,' said one of them. 'There's two coloured-glass windows in the chapel presented by the last Governor's widow. Lovely they are, St Peter and St Paul in prison being released by an angel. Some of the Low Church prisoners don't like them, though.

'We had a lecture last week, too, but it wasn't very popular – "The Work of the League of Nations", given by a young chap of the name of Potts. Still, it makes a change. I hear you've been having a lot of changes at Blackstone.'

'I should just about think we have,' said one of the convicts, and proceeded to give a somewhat exaggerated account of the death of Mr Prendergast.

Presently one of the warders, observing that Paul seemed shy of joining in the conversation, handed him a daily paper. 'Like to look at this, sonny?' he said. 'It's the last you'll see for some time.'

There was very little in it to interest Paul, whose only information from the outside world during the last six weeks had come from Sir Wilfred Lucas-Dockery's weekly bulletins (for one of the first discoveries of his captivity was that interest in 'news' does not spring from genuine curiosity, but from the desire for completeness. During his long years of freedom he had scarcely allowed a day to pass without reading fairly fully from at least two newspapers, always pressing on with a series of events which never came to an end. Once the series was broken he had little desire to resume it), but he was deeply moved to discover on one of the middle plates an obscure but recognizable photograph of Margot and Peter. 'The Honourable Mrs Beste-Chetwynde,' it said below, 'and her son, Peter, who succeeds his uncle as Earl of Pastmaster.' In the next column was an announcement of the death of Lord Pastmaster and a brief survey of his uneventful life. At the end it said, 'It is understood that Mrs Beste-Chetwynde and the young Earl, who have been spending the last few months at their villa in Corfu, will return to England in a few days. Mrs Beste-Chetwynde has for many years been a prominent hostess in the fashionable world and is regarded as one of the most beautiful women in Society. Her son's succession to the earl-dom recalls the sensation caused in May of this year by the

announcement of her engagement to Mr Paul Pennyfeather
and the dramatic arrest of the bridegroom at a leading West
End hotel a few hours before the wedding ceremony. The new
Lord Pastmaster is sixteen years old, and has up till now been
educated privately.'

Paul sat back in the carriage for a long time looking at the
photograph, while his companions played several hands of
poker in reckless disregard of Standing Orders. In his six weeks
of solitude and grave consideration he had failed to make up
his mind about Margot Beste-Chetwynde; it was torn and
distracted by two conflicting methods of thought. On one side
was the dead weight of precept, inherited from generations of
schoolmasters and divines. According to these, the problem
was difficult but not insoluble. He had 'done the right thing'
in shielding the woman: so much was clear, but Margot had
not quite filled the place assigned to her, for in this case she
was grossly culpable, and he was shielding her, not from
misfortune nor injustice, but from the consequence of her
crimes; he felt a flush about his knees as Boy Scout honour
whispered that Margot had got him into a row and ought jolly
well to own up and face the music. As he sat over his post-bags
he had wrestled with this argument without achieving any
satisfactory result except a growing conviction that there was
something radically inapplicable about this whole code of
ready-made honour that is the still small voice, trained to
command, of the Englishman all the world over. On the other
hand was the undeniable cogency of Peter Beste-Chetwynde's
'You can't see Mamma in prison, can you?' The more Paul
considered this, the more he perceived it to be the statement
of a natural law. He appreciated the assumption of comprehen-
sion with which Peter had delivered it. As he studied Margot's
photograph, dubiously transmitted as it was, he was streng-
thened in his belief that there was, in fact, and should be, one
law for her and another for himself, and that the raw little
exertions of nineteenth-century Radicals were essentially
base and trivial and misdirected. It was not simply that Margot
had been very rich or that he had been in love with her. It

was just that he saw the *impossibility* of Margot in prison; the
bare connexion of vocables associating the ideas was obscene.
Margot dressed in prison uniform, hustled down corridors
by wardresses – all like the younger Miss Fagan – visited
by philanthropic old ladies with devotional pamphlets, set to
work in the laundry washing the other prisoners' clothes –
these things were *impossible*, and if the preposterous processes
of law had condemned her, then the woman that they actually caught and pinned down would not have been Margot,
but some quite other person of the same name and somewhat similar appearance. It was impossible to imprison the
Margot who had committed the crime. If some one had to
suffer that the public might be discouraged from providing
poor Mrs Grimes with the only employment for which civilization had prepared her, then it had better be Paul than
that other woman with Margot's name, for anyone who has
been to an English public school will always feel comparatively
at home in prison. It is the people brought up in the gay
intimacy of the slums, Paul learned, who find prison so soul-
destroying.

How lovely Margot was, Paul reflected, even in this absurd
photograph, this grey-and-black smudge of ink! Even the
most hardened criminal there – he was serving his third sentence for blackmail – laid down his cards for a moment and
remarked upon how the whole carriage seemed to be flooded
with the delectable savour of the Champs-Élysées in early June.
'Funny,' he said. 'I thought I smelt scent.' And that set them
off talking about women.

*

Paul found another old friend at Egdon Heath Prison: a short,
thick-set, cheerful figure who stumped along in front of him
on the way to chapel, making a good deal of noise with an
artificial leg. 'Here we are again, old boy!' he remarked during
one of the responses. 'I'm in the soup as per usual.'

'Didn't you like the job?' Paul asked.

'Top hole,' said Grimes, 'but the hell of a thing happened. Tell you later.'

That morning, complete with pickaxes, field-telephone, and two armed and mounted warders, Paul and a little squad of fellow-criminals were led to the quarries. Grimes was in the party.

'I've been here a fortnight,' said Grimes as soon as they got an opportunity of talking, 'and it seems too long already. I've always been a sociable chap, and I don't like it. Three years is too long, old boy. Still, we'll have God's own beano when I get out. I've been thinking about that day and night.'

'I suppose it was bigamy?' said Paul.

'The same. I ought to have stayed abroad. I was arrested as soon as I landed. You see, Mrs Grimes turned up at the shop, so off Grimes went. There are various sorts of hell, but that young woman can beat up a pretty lively one of her own.'

A warder passed them by, and they moved apart, banging industriously at the sandstone cliff before them.

'I'm not sure it wasn't worth it, though,' said Grimes, 'to see poor old Flossie in the box and my sometime father-in-law. I hear the old man's shut down the school. Grimes gave the place a bad name. See anything of old Prendy ever?'

'He was murdered the other day.'

'Poor old Prendy! He wasn't cut out for the happy life, was he? D'you know, I think I shall give up schoolmastering for good when I get out. It doesn't lead anywhere.'

'It seems to have led us both to the same place.'

'Yes, rather a coincidence, isn't it? Damn, here's that policeman again.'

Soon they were marched back to the prison. Except for the work in the quarries, life at Egdon was almost the same as at Blackstone.

'Slops outside,' chapel, privacy.

After a week, however, Paul became conscious of an alien influence at work. His first intimation of this came from the Chaplain.

'Your library books,' he said one day, popping cheerfully in Paul's cell and handing him two new novels, still in their wrappers, and bearing inside them the label of a Piccadilly bookseller. 'If you don't like them I have several for you to choose from.' He showed him rather coyly the pile of gaily-bound volumes he carried under his arm. 'I thought you'd like the new Virginia Woolf. It's only been out two days.'

'Thank you, sir,' said Paul politely. Clearly the library of his new prison was run on a much more enterprising and extravagant plan than at Blackstone.

'Or there's this book on Theatrical Design,' said the Chaplain, showing him a large illustrated volume that could hardly have cost less than three guineas. 'Perhaps we might stretch a point and give you that as well as your "education work".'

'Thank you, sir,' said Paul.

'Let me know if you want a change,' said the Chaplain. 'And, by the way, you're allowed to write a letter now, you know. If, by any chance, you're writing to Mrs Beste-Chetwynde, do mention that you think the library good. She's presenting a new pulpit to the chapel in carved alabaster,' he added irrelevantly, and popped out again to give Grimes a copy of Smiles' *Self-Help*, out of which some unreceptive reader in the remote past had torn the last hundred and eight pages.

'People may think as they like about well-thumbed favourites,' thought Paul, 'but there is something incomparably thrilling in first opening a brand-new book. Why should the Chaplain want me to mention the library to Margot?' he wondered.

That evening at supper Paul noticed without surprise that there were several small pieces of coal in his dripping: that kind of thing did happen now and then; but he was somewhat disconcerted, when he attempted to scrape them out, to find that they were quite soft. Prison food was often rather odd; it was a mistake to complain; but still . . . He examined his dripping more closely. It had a pinkish tinge that should not have been there and was unusually firm and sticky under his knife. He tasted it dubiously. It was *pâté de foie gras*.

From then onwards there was seldom a day on which some small meteorite of this kind did not mysteriously fall from the outside world. One day he returned from the heath to find his cell heavy with scent in the half-dark, for the lights were rarely lit until some time after sundown, and the window was very small. His table was filled with a large bunch of winter roses, which had cost three shillings each that morning in Bond Street. (Prisoners at Egdon are allowed to keep flowers in their cells, and often risk severe reprimand by stooping to pick pimpernels and periwinkles on their way from work.)

On another occasion the prison-doctor, trotting on his daily round of inspection, paused at Paul's cell, examined his name on the card hanging inside his door, looked hard at him and said, 'You need a tonic.' He trotted on without more ado, but next day a huge medicine-bottle was placed in Paul's cell. 'You're to take two glasses with each meal,' said the warder, 'and I hopes you like it.' Paul could not quite decide whether the warder's tone was friendly or not, but he liked the medicine, for it was brown sherry.

On another occasion great indignation was aroused in the cell next door to him, whose occupant – an aged burglar – was inadvertently given Paul's ration of caviare. He was speed- ily appeased by the substitution for it of an unusually large lump of cold bacon, but not before the warder in charge had suffered considerable alarm at the possibility of a complaint to the Governor.

'I'm not one to make a fuss really,' said the old burglar, 'but I will be treated fair. Why, you only had to look at the stuff they give to me to see that it was bad, let alone taste it. And on bacon night, too! You take my tip,' he said to Paul as they found themselves alone in the quarries one day, 'and keep your eyes open. You're a new one, and they might easily try and put a thing like that over on you. Don't eat it; that's putting you in the wrong. Keep it and show it to the Governor. They ain't got no right to try on a thing like that, and they knows it.'

Presently a letter came from Margot. It was not a long one.

Dear Paul, it said,

It is so difficult writing to you because, you know, I never can write letters, and it's so particularly hard with you because the policemen read it and cross it all out if they don't like it, and I can't really think of anything they will like. Peter and I are back at King's Thursday. It was divine at Corfu, except for an English Doctor who was a bore and would call so often. Do you know, I don't really like this house terribly, and I am having it redone. Do you mind? Peter has become an earl — did you know? — and is rather sweet about it, and very self-conscious, which you wouldn't expect, really, would you, knowing Peter? I'm going to come and see you some time — may I? — when I can get away, but Bobby P.'s death has made such a lot of things to see to. I do hope you're getting enough food and books and things, or will they cross that out? Love, Margot. I was cut by Lady Circumference, my dear, at Newmarket, a real point-blank Tranby Croft cut. Poor Maltravers says if I'm not careful I shall find myself socially ostracized. Don't you think that will be marvellous? I may be wrong, but, d'you know, I rather believe poor little Alastair Trumpington's going to fall in love with me. What shall I do?

*

Eventually Margot came herself.

It was the first time they had met since the morning in June when she had sent him off to rescue her distressed protégées in Marseilles. The meeting took place in a small room set aside for visitors. Margot sat at one end of the table, Paul at the other, with a warder between them.

'I must ask you both to put your hands on the table in front of you,' said the warder.

'Like Up Jenkins,' said Margot faintly, laying her exquisitely manicured hands with the gloves beside her bag. Paul for the first time noticed how coarse and ill-kept his hands had become. For a moment neither spoke.

'Do I look awful?' Paul said at last. 'I haven't seen a looking-glass for some time.'

'Well, perhaps just a little *mal soigné*, darling. Don't they let you shave at all?'

'No discussion of the prison *régime* is permitted. Prisoners are allowed to make a plain statement of their state of health but must on no account make complaints or comments upon their general condition.'

'O dear!' said Margot; 'this is going to be very difficult. What are we to say to each other? I'm almost sorry I came. You are glad I came, aren't you?'

'Don't mind me, mum, if you wants to talk personal,' said the warder kindly. 'I only has to stop conspiracy. Nothing I hears ever goes any farther, and I hears a good deal, I can tell you. They carry on awful, some of the women, what with crying and fainting and hysterics generally. Why, one of them,' he said with relish, 'had an epileptic fit not long ago.'

'I think it's more than likely I shall have a fit,' said Margot. 'I've never felt so shy in my life. Paul, *do* say something, please.'

'How's Alastair?' said Paul.

'Rather sweet, really. He's always at King's Thursday now. I like him.'

Another pause.

'Do you know,' said Margot, 'it's an odd thing, but I do believe that after all these years I'm beginning to be regarded as no longer a respectable woman. I told you when I wrote, didn't I, that Lady Circumference cut me the other day? Of course she's just a thoroughly bad-mannered old woman, but there have been a whole lot of things rather like that lately. Don't you think it's rather awful?'

'You won't mind much, will you?' said Paul. 'They're awful old bores, anyway.'

'Yes, but I don't like *them* dropping *me*. Of course, I don't mind, really, but I think it's just a pity, particularly for Peter. It's not just Lady Circumference, but Lady Vanburgh and Fanny Simpleforth and the Stayles and all those people. It's a pity it should happen just when Peter's beginning to be a little class-conscious, anyway. It'll give him all the wrong ideas, don't you think?'

'How's business?' asked Paul abruptly.

'Paul, you mustn't be nasty to me,' said Margot in a low voice. 'I don't think you'd say that if you knew quite how I was feeling.'

'I'm sorry, Margot. As a matter of fact, I just wanted to know.'

'I'm selling out. A Swiss firm was making things difficult. But I don't think that business has anything to do with the – the ostracism, as Maltravers would say. I believe it's all because I'm beginning to grow old.'

'I never heard anything so ridiculous. Why, all those people are about eighty, and anyway, you aren't at all.'

'I was afraid you wouldn't understand,' said Margot, and there was another pause.

'Ten minutes more,' said the warder.

'Things haven't turned out quite as we expected them to, have they?' said Margot.

They talked about some parties Margot had been to and the books Paul was reading. At last Margot said: 'Paul, I'm going. I simply can't stand another moment of this.'

'It was nice of you to come,' said Paul.

'I've decided something rather important,' said Margot, 'just this minute. I am going to be married quite soon to Maltravers. I'm sorry, but I am.'

'I suppose it's because I look so awful?' said Paul.

'No, it's just everything. It's that, too, in a way, but not the way you mean, Paul. It's simply something that's going to happen. Do you understand at all, dear? It may help you, too, in a way, but I don't want you to think that that's the reason, either. It's just how things are going to happen. Oh dear! How difficult it is to say anything.'

'If you should want to kiss good-bye,' said the gaoler, 'not being husband and wife, it's not usual. Still, I don't mind stretching a point for once . . .'

'Oh, God!' said Margot, and left the room without looking back.

Paul returned to his cell. His supper had already been served out to him, a small pie from which protruded the feet of two pigeons; there was even a table-napkin wrapped round it. But Paul had very little appetite, for he was greatly pained at how little he was pained by the events of the afternoon.

CHAPTER V
The Passing of a Public School Man

A DAY or two later Paul found himself next to Grimes in the quarry. When the warder was out of earshot Grimes said: 'Old boy, I can't stand this much longer. It just ain't good enough.'

'I don't see any way out,' said Paul. 'Anyway, it's quite bearable. I'd as soon be here as at Llanabba.'

'Not so Grimes,' said Grimes. 'He just languishes in captivity, like the lark. It's all right for you – you like reading and thinking and all that. Well, I'm different, you know. I like drink and a bit of fun, and chatting now and then to my pals. I'm a sociable chap. It's turning me into a giddy machine, this life, and there's an awful chaplain, who gives me the pip, who keeps butting in in a breezy kind of way and asking if I feel I'm "right with God". Of course I'm not, and I tell him so. I can stand most sorts of misfortune, old boy, but I can't stand repression. That was what broke me up at Llanabba, and it's what's going to break me up here, if I don't look out for myself. It seems to me it's time Grimes flitted off to another clime.'

'No one has ever succeeded in escaping from this prison,' said Paul.

'Well, just you watch next time there's a fog!'

As luck would have it, there was a fog next day, a heavy impenetrable white mist which came up quite suddenly while they were at work, enveloping men and quarry in the way that mists do on Egdon Heath.

'Close up there,' said the warder in charge. 'Stop work and close up. Look out there, you idiot!' for Grimes had stumbled over the field-telephone. 'If you've broken it you'll come up before the Governor to-morrow.'

'Hold this horse,' said the other warder, handing the reins to Grimes.

He stooped and began to collect the chains on which the men were strung for their march home. Grimes seemed to be having some difficulty with the horse, which was plunging and rearing farther away from the squad. 'Can't you even hold a horse?' said the warder. Suddenly Grimes, with remarkable agility considering his leg, was seen to be in the saddle riding away into the heath.

'Come back,' roared the warder, 'come back, or I'll fire.' He put his rifle to his shoulder and fired into the fog. 'He'll come back all right,' he said. 'No one ever gets away for long. He'll get solitary confinement and No. 1 diet for this, poor fish.'

No one seemed to be much disturbed by the incident, even when it was found that the field-telephone was disconnected.

'He hasn't a hope,' said the warder. 'They often do that, just put down their tools sudden and cut and run. But they can't get away in those clothes and with no money. We shall warn all the farms to-night. Sometimes they stays out hiding for several days, but back they comes when they're hungry, or else they get arrested the moment they shows up in a village. I reckon it's just nerves makes them try it.'

That evening the horse came back, but there was no sign of Grimes. Special patrols were sent out with bloodhounds straining at their leashes; the farms and villages on the heath were warned, and the anxious inhabitants barred their doors closely and more pertinently forbade their children to leave the house on any pretext whatever; the roads were watched for miles, and all cars were stopped and searched, to the intense annoyance of many law-abiding citizens. But Grimes did not turn up. Bets were slyly made among the prisoners as to the day of his recovery; but days passed, and the rations of bread changed hands, but still there was no Grimes.

A week later at morning-service the Chaplain prayed for his soul: the Governor crossed his name off the Body Receipt Book and notified the Home Secretary, the Right Honourable Sir Humphrey Maltravers, that Grimes was dead.

'I'm afraid it was a terrible end,' said the Chaplain to Paul.

'Did they find the body?'

'No, that is the worst thing about it. The hounds followed his scent as far as Egdon Mire; there it ended. A shepherd who knows the paths through the bog found his hat floating on the surface at the most treacherous part. I'm afraid there is no doubt that he died a very horrible death.'

'Poor old Grimes!' said Paul. 'And he was an old Harrovian, too.'

But later, thinking things over as he ate peacefully, one by one, the oysters that had been provided as a 'relish' for his supper, Paul knew that Grimes was not dead. Lord Tangent was dead; Mr Prendergast was dead; the time would even come for Paul Pennyfeather; but Grimes, Paul at last realized, was of the immortals. He was a life force. Sentenced to death in Flanders, he popped up in Wales; drowned in Wales, he emerged in South America; engulfed in the dark mystery of Egdon Mire, he would rise again somewhere at some time, shaking from his limbs the musty integuments of the tomb. Surely he had followed in the Bacchic train of distant Arcady, and played on the reeds of myth by forgotten streams, and taught the childish satyrs the art of love? Had he not suffered unscathed the fearful dooms of all the offended gods, of all the histories, fire, brimstone, and yawning earthquakes, plague, and pestilence? Had he not stood, like the Pompeiian sentry, while the Citadels of the Plain fell to ruin about his ears? Had he not, like some grease-caked Channel-swimmer, breasted the waves of the Deluge? Had he not moved unseen when the darkness covered the waters?

'I often wonder whether I am blameless in the matter,' said the Chaplain. 'It is awful to think of someone under my care having come to so terrible an end. I tried to console him and reconcile him with his life, but things are so difficult; there are so many men to see. Poor fellow! To think of him alone out there in the bog, with no one to help him!'

CHAPTER VI
The Passing of Paul Pennyfeather

A FEW days later Paul was summoned to the Governor's room.

'I have an order here from the Home Secretary granting leave for you to go into a private nursing-home for the removal of your appendix. You will start under escort, in plain clothes, this morning.'

'But, sir,' said Paul, 'I don't want to have my appendix removed. In fact, it was done years ago when I was still at school.'

'Nonsense!' said the Governor. 'I've got an order here from the Home Secretary especially requiring that it shall be done. Officer, take this man away and give him his clothes for the journey.'

Paul was led away. The clothes in which he had been tried had been sent with him from Blackstone. The warder took them out of a locker, unfolded them and handed them to Paul. 'Shoes, socks, trousers, waistcoat, coat, shirt, collar, tie, and hat,' he said. 'Will you sign for them? The jewellery stays here.' He collected the watch, links, tie-pin, note-case, and the other odds and ends that had been in Paul's pockets and put them back in the locker. 'We can't do anything about your hair,' said the warder, 'but you're allowed a shave.'

Half an hour later Paul emerged from his cell, looking for all the world like a normal civilized man, such as you might see daily in any tube-railway.

'Feels funny, don't it?' said the warder who let him out. 'Here's your escort.'

Another normal civilized man, such as you might see daily in any tube-railway, confronted Paul.

'Time we started, if you're quite ready,' he said. Robbed of their uniforms, it seemed natural that they should treat each other with normal consideration. Indeed, Paul thought he detected a certain deference in the man's tone.

'It's very odd,' said Paul in the van that took them to the station; 'it's no good arguing with the Governor, but he's made some ridiculous mistake. I've had my appendix out already.'

'Not half,' said the warder with a wink, 'but don't go talking about it so loud. The driver's not in on this.'

A first-class carriage had been reserved for them in the train. As they drew out of Egdon Station the warder said: 'Well, that's the last you'll see of the old place for some time. Solemn thought, death, ain't it?' And he gave another shattering wink.

They had luncheon in their carriage, Paul feeling a little too shy of his closely-cropped head to venture hatless into the restaurant car. After luncheon they smoked cigars. The warder paid from a fat note-case. 'Oh, I nearly forgot,' he said. 'Here's your will for you to sign, in case anything should happen.' He produced a long blue paper and handed it to Paul. *The Last Will and Testament of Paul Pennyfeather* was handsomely engrossed at the top. Below, it was stated, with the usual legal periphrases, that he left all he possessed to Margot Beste-Chetwynde. Two witnesses had already signed below the vacant space. 'I'm sure this is all very irregular,' said Paul signing;

'I wish you'd tell me what all this means.'

'I don't know nothing,' said the warder. 'The young gentleman give me the will.'

'What young gentleman?'

'How should I know?' said the warder. 'The young gentleman what's arranged everything. Very sensible to make a will. You never know with an operation what may happen, do you? I had an aunt died having gallstones taken out, and she hadn't made a will. Very awkward it was, her not being married properly, you see. Fine healthy woman, too, to look at her. Don't you get worried, Mr Pennyfeather; everything will be done strictly according to regulations.'

'Where are we going? At least you must know that.'

For answer the warder took a printed card from his pocket. *Cliff Place, Worthing*, he read. *High-class Nursing and Private Sanatorium. Electric thermal treatment under medical supervision. Augus-*

tus Fagan, M.D., Proprietor. 'Approved by the Home Secretary,' said the warder. 'Nothing to complain of.'

Later in the afternoon they arrived. A car was waiting to take them to Cliff Place.

'This ends my responsibility,' said the warder. 'From now on the doctor's in charge.'

*

Like all Dr Fagan's enterprises, Cliff Place was conceived on a large scale. The house stood alone on the seashore some miles from the town, and was approached by a long drive. In detail, however, it showed some signs of neglect. The veranda was deep in driven leaves; two of the windows were broken. Paul's escort rang the bell at the front door, and Dingy, dressed as a nurse, opened it to them.

'The servants have all gone,' she said. 'I suppose this is the appendicitis case. Come in.' She showed no signs of recognizing Paul as she led him upstairs. 'This is your room. The Home Office regulations insisted that it should be on an upper storey with barred windows. We have had to put the bars in specially. They will be charged for in the bill. The surgeon will be here in a few minutes.'

As she went out she locked the door. Paul sat down on the bed and waited. Below his window the sea beat on the shingle. A small steam-yacht lay at anchor some distance out to sea. The grey horizon faded indistinctly into the grey sky.

Presently steps approached, and his door opened. In came Dr Fagan, Sir Alastair Digby-Vane-Trumpington, and an elderly little man with a drooping red moustache, evidently much the worse for drink.

'Sorry we're late,' said Sir Alastair, 'but I've had an awful day with this man trying to keep him sober. He gave me the slip just as we were starting. I was afraid at first that he was too tight to be moved, but I think he can just carry on. Have you got the papers made out?'

No one paid much attention to Paul.

'Here they are,' said Dr Fagan. 'This is the statement you are to forward to the Home Secretary, and a duplicate for the Governor of the prison. Shall I read them to you?'

' 'Sh'all right!' said the surgeon.

'They merely state that you operated on the patient for appendicitis, but that he died under the anaesthetic without regaining consciousness.'

'Poor ole chap!' said the surgeon. 'Poor, poor l'il girl!' And two tears of sympathy welled up in his eyes. 'I daresay the world had been very hard on her. It's a hard world for women.'

'That's all right,' said Sir Alastair. 'Don't worry. You did all that was humanly possible.'

'That's the truth,' said the surgeon, 'and I don't care who knows it.'

'This is the ordinary certificate of death,' said Dr Fagan. 'Will you be so good as to sign it there?'

'Oh, death, where is thy sting-a-ling-a-ling?' said the surgeon, and with these words and a laboured effort of the pen he terminated the legal life of Paul Pennyfeather.

'Splendid!' said Sir Alastair. 'Now here's your money. If I were you I should run off and have a drink while the pubs are still open.'

'D'you know, I think I will,' said the surgeon, and left the sanatorium.

There was a hush for nearly a minute after he had left the room. The presence of death, even in its coldest and most legal form, seemed to cause an air of solemnity. It was broken at length by the arrival of Flossie, splendidly attired in magenta and green.

'Why, here you all are!' she said with genuine delight. 'And Mr Pennyfeather, too, to be sure! Quite a little party!'

She had said the right thing. The word 'party' seemed to strike a responsive note in Dr Fagan.

'Let us go down to supper,' he said. 'I'm sure we all have a great deal to be thankful for.'

*

After supper Dr Fagan made a little speech. 'I think this an important evening for most of us,' he said, 'most of all for my dear friend and sometime colleague Paul Pennyfeather, in whose death to-night we are all to some extent participants. For myself as well as for him it is the beginning of a new phase of life. Frankly, this nursing-home has not been a success. A time must come to every man when he begins to doubt his vocation. You may think me almost an old man, but I do not feel too old to start lightheartedly on a new manner of life. This evening's events have made this possible for me. I think,' he said, glancing at his daughters, 'that it is time I was alone. But this is not the hour to review the plans of my future. When you get to my age, if you have been at all observant of the people you have met and the accidents which have happened to you, you cannot help being struck with an amazing cohesiveness of events. How promiscuously we who are here this evening have been thrown together! How enduring and endearing the memories that from now onwards will unite us! I think we should drink a toast – to Fortune, a much-maligned lady.'

Once before Paul had drunk the same toast. This time there was no calamity. They drank silently, and Alastair rose from the table.

'It's time Paul and I were going,' he said.

They walked down to the beach together. A boat was waiting for them.

'That's Margot's yacht,' said Alastair. 'It's to take you to her house at Corfu until you've decided about things. Good-bye. Good luck!'

'Aren't you coming any farther?' asked Paul.

'No, I've got to drive back to King's Thursday. Margot will be anxious to know how things have gone off.'

Paul got into the boat and was rowed away. Sir Alastair, like Sir Bedivere, watched him out of sight.

CHAPTER VII
Resurrection

THREE weeks later Paul sat on the veranda of Margot's villa, with his evening *apéritif* before him, watching the sunset on the Albanian hills across the water change, with the crude brilliance of a German picture-postcard, from green to violet. He looked at his watch, which had that morning arrived from England. It was half-past six.

Below him in the harbour a ship had come in from Greece and was unloading her cargo. The little boats hung round her like flies, plying their trade of olive-wood souvenirs and forged francs. There were two hours before dinner. Paul rose and descended the arcaded street into the square, drawing his scarf tight about his throat; the evenings began to get cold about this time. It was odd being dead. That morning Margot had sent him a bunch of Press cuttings about himself, most of them headed 'Wedding Sensation Echo' or 'Death of Society Bridegroom Convict'. With them were his tie-pin and the rest of his possessions which had been sent to her from Egdon. He felt the need of the bustle at the cafés and the quayside to convince him fully of his existence. He stopped at a stall and bought some Turkish delight. It was odd being dead.

Suddenly he was aware of a familiar figure approaching him across the square.

'Hullo!' said Paul.

'Hullo!' said Otto Silenus. He was carrying on his shoulder a shapeless knapsack of canvas.

'Why don't you give that to one of the boys? They'll take it for a few drachmas.'

'I have no money. Will you pay him?'

'Yes.'

'All right! Then that will be best. I suppose you are staying with Margot?'

'I'm staying at her house. She's in England.'

'That's a pity. I hoped I should find her here. Still I will stay for a little, I think. Will there be room for me?'

'I suppose so. I'm all alone here.'

'I have changed my mind. I think, after all, I will marry Margot.'

'I'm afraid it's too late.'

'Too late?'

'Yes, she married someone else.'

'I never thought of that. Oh well, it doesn't matter really. Whom did she marry? That sensible Maltravers?'

'Yes, he's changed his name now. He's called Viscount Metroland.'

'What a funny name!'

They walked up the hill together. 'I've just been to Greece to see the buildings there,' said Professor Silenus.

'Did you like them?'

'They are unspeakably ugly. But there were some nice goats. I thought they sent you to prison.'

'Yes, they did, but I got out.'

'Yes, you must have, I suppose. Wasn't it nice?'

'Not terribly.'

'Funny! I thought it would suit you so well. You never can tell with people, can you, what's going to suit them?'

Margot's servants did not seem surprised at the arrival of another guest.

'I think I shall stay here a long time,' said Professor Silenus after dinner. 'I have no money left. Are you going soon?'

'Yes, I'm going back to Oxford again to learn theology.'

'That will be a good thing. You used not to have a moustache, used you?' he asked after a time.

'No,' said Paul. 'I'm just growing one now. I don't want people to recognize me when I go back to England.'

'I think it's uglier,' said Professor Silenus. 'Well, I must go to bed.'

'Have you slept any better lately?'

'Twice since I saw you. It's about my average. Good night.'

Ten minutes later he came back on to the terrace, wearing silk pyjamas and a tattered old canvas dressing-gown.

'Can you lend me a nail file?' he asked.

'There's one on my dressing-table.'

'Thank you.' But he did not go. Instead he walked to the parapet and leant out, looking across the sea. 'It's a good thing for you to be a clergyman,' he said at last. 'People get ideas about a thing they call life. It sets them all wrong. I think it's poets that are responsible chiefly. Shall I tell you about life?'

'Yes, do,' said Paul politely.

'Well, it's like the big wheel at Luna Park. Have you seen the big wheel?'

'No, I'm afraid not.'

'You pay five francs and go into a room with tiers of seats all round, and in the centre the floor is made of a great disc of polished wood that revolves quickly. At first you sit down and watch the others. They are all trying to sit in the wheel, and they keep getting flung off, and that makes them laugh, and you laugh too. It's great fun.'

'I don't think that sounds very much like life,' said Paul rather sadly.

'Oh, but it is, though. You see, the nearer you can get to the hub of the wheel the slower it is moving and the easier it is to stay on. There's generally someone in the centre who stands up and sometimes does a sort of dance. Often he's paid by the management, though, or, at any rate, he's allowed in free. Of course at the very centre there's a point completely at rest, if one could only find it: I'm not sure I am not very near that point myself. Of course the professional men get in the way. Lots of people just enjoy scrambling on and being whisked off and scrambling on again. How they all shriek and giggle! Then there are others, like Margot, who sit as far out as they can and hold on for dear life and enjoy that. But the whole point about the wheel is that you needn't get on it at all, if you don't want to. People get hold of ideas about life, and that makes them think they've got to join in the game, even if they don't enjoy it. It doesn't suit everyone.

'People don't see that when they say "life" they mean two different things. They can mean simply existence, with its physiological implications of growth and organic change. They can't escape that – even by death, but because that's inevitable they think the other idea of life is too – the scrambling and excitement and bumps and the effort to get to the middle, and when we do get to the middle, it's just as if we never started. It's so odd.

'Now you're a person who was clearly meant to stay in the seats and sit still and if you get bored watch the others. Somehow you got on to the wheel, and you got thrown off again at once with a hard bump. It's all right for Margot, who can cling on, and for me, at the centre, but you're static. Instead of this absurd division into sexes they ought to class people as static and dynamic. There's a real distinction there, though I can't tell you how it comes. I think we're probably two quite different species spiritually.

'I used that idea of the wheel in a cinema-film once. I think it rather sounds like it, don't you? What was it I came back for?'

'A nail file.'

'Oh yes, of course. I know of no more utterly boring and futile occupation than generalizing about life. Did you take in what I was saying?'

'Yes, I think so.'

'I think I shall have my meals alone in future. Will you tell the servants? It makes me feel quite ill to talk so much. Good night.'

'Good night,' said Paul.

*

Some months later Paul returned to Scone College after the absence of little more than a year. His death, though depriving him of his certificates, left him his knowledge. He sat successfully for smalls and Matriculation and entered his old college once more, wearing a commoner's gown and a heavy cavalry moustache. This and his natural diffidence formed a complete disguise. Nobody recognized him. After much doubt and deliberation he retained the name of Pennyfeather, explaining to the Chaplain that he had, he believed, had a distant cousin at Scone a short time ago.

'He came to a very sad end,' said the Chaplain, 'a wild young man.'

'He was a *very* distant cousin,' said Paul hastily.

'Yes, yes, I am sure he was. There is no resemblance between you. He was a thoroughly degenerate type, I am afraid.'

Paul's scout also remembered the name.

'There used to be another Mr Pennyfeather on this staircase once,' he said, 'a very queer gentleman indeed. Would you believe it, sir, he used to take off all his clothes and go out and dance in the quad at night. Nice quiet gentleman, too, he was, except for his dancing. He must have been a little queer in his head, I suppose. I don't know what became of him. They say he died in prison.' Then he proceeded to tell Paul about an Annamese student who had attempted to buy one of the Senior Tutor's daughters.

On the second Sunday of term the Chaplain asked Paul to breakfast. 'It's a sad thing,' he said, 'the way that the 'Varsity breakfast − "brekker" we used to call it in my day − is dying out. People haven't time for it. Always off to lectures at nine o'clock, except on Sundays. Have another kidney, won't you?'

There was another don present, called Mr Sniggs, who addressed the Chaplain rather superciliously, Paul thought, as 'Padre'.

There was also an undergraduate from another college, a theological student called Stubbs, a grave young man with a quiet voice and with carefully formed opinions. He had a little argument with Mr Sniggs about the plans for rebuilding the Bodleian. Paul supported him.

Next day Paul found Stubbs' card on his table, the corner turned up. Paul went to Hertford to call on Stubbs, but found him out. He left his card, the corner turned up. Two days later a little note came from Hertford:

Dear Pennyfeather,

I wonder if you would care to come to tea next Tuesday, to meet the College Secretary of the League of Nations Union and the Chaplain of the Oxford prison. It would be so nice if you could.

Paul went and ate honey buns and anchovy toast. He liked the ugly, subdued little College, and he liked Stubbs.

As term went on Paul and Stubbs took to going for walks together, over Mesopotamia to Old Marston and Beckley. One afternoon, quite lighthearted at the fresh weather, and their long walk, and their tea, Stubbs signed *Randall Cantuar* in the visitors' book.

Paul rejoined the League of Nations Union and the O.S.C.U. On one occasion he and Stubbs and some other friends went to the prison to visit the criminals there and sing part-songs to them.

'It opens the mind,' said Stubbs, 'to see all sides of life. How those unfortunate men appreciated our singing!'

One day in Blackwell's bookshop Paul found a stout volume, which, the assistant told him, was rapidly becoming a bestseller. It was called *Mother Wales*, by *Augustus Fagan*. Paul bought it and took it back with him. Stubbs had already read it.

'Most illuminating,' he said. 'The hospital statistics are terrible. Do you think it would be a good idea to organize a joint debate with Jesus on the subject?' The book was dedicated '*To my wife, a wedding present*'. It was eloquently written. When he had read it Paul put it on his shelves next to Dean Stanley's *Eastern Church*.

One other incident recalled momentarily Paul's past life.

One day at the beginning of his second year, as Paul and Stubbs were bicycling down the High as from one lecture to another, they nearly ran into an open Rolls-Royce that swung out of Oriel Street at a dangerous speed. In the back, a heavy fur rug over his knees, sat Philbrick. He turned round as he passed and waved a gloved hand to Paul over the hood.

'Hullo!' he said; 'hullo! How are you! Come and look me up one day. I'm living on the river – Skindle's.'

Then the car disappeared down the High Street, and Paul went on to the lecture.

'Who was your opulent friend?' asked Stubbs, rather impressed.

'Arnold Bennett,' said Paul.

'I thought I knew his face,' said Stubbs.

Then the lecturer came in, arranged his papers, and began a lucid exposition of the heresies of the second century. There was a bishop of Bithynia, Paul learned, who had denied the Divinity of Christ, the immortality of the soul, the existence of good, the legality of marriage, and the validity of the Sacrament of Extreme Unction. How right they had been to condemn him!

EPILOGUE

IT was Paul's third year of uneventful residence at Scone. Stubbs finished his cocoa, knocked out his pipe and rose to go. 'I must be off to my digs,' he said. 'You're lucky staying in college. It's a long ride back to Walton Street on a night like this.'

'D'you want to take Von Hugel?' asked Paul.

'No, not to-night. May I leave it till to-morrow?'

Stubbs picked up his scholar's gown and wrapped it round his shoulders. 'That was an interesting paper to-night about the Polish plebiscites.'

'Yes, wasn't it?' said Paul.

Outside there was a confused roaring and breaking of glass.

'The Bollinger seem to be enjoying themselves,' said Paul. 'Whose rooms are they in this time?'

'Pastmaster's, I think. That young man seems to be going a bit fast for his age.'

'Well, I hope he enjoys it,' said Paul. 'Good night.'

'Good night, Paul,' said Stubbs.

Paul put the chocolate biscuits back in the cupboard, refilled his pipe, and settled down in his chair.

Presently he heard footsteps and a knock at his door.

'Come in,' he said, looking round.

Peter Pastmaster came into the room. He was dressed in the bottle-green and white evening coat of the Bollinger Club. His face was flushed and his dark hair slightly disordered.

'May I come in?'

'Yes, do.'

'Have you got a drink?'

'You seem to have had a good many already.'

'I've had the Boller in my rooms. Noisy lot. Oh, hell! I must have a drink.'

'There's some whisky in the cupboard. You're drinking rather a lot these days, aren't you, Peter?'

Peter said nothing, but helped himself to some whisky and soda.

'Feeling a bit ill,' he said. Then, after a pause, 'Paul, why have you been cutting me all this time?'

'I don't know. I didn't think there was much to be gained by our knowing each other.'

'Not angry about anything?'

'No, why should I be?'

'Oh, I don't know.' Peter turned his glass in his hand, staring at it intently. 'I've been rather angry with you, you know.'

'Why?'

'Oh, I don't know – about Margot and the man Maltravers and everything.'

'I don't think I was much to blame.'

'No, I suppose not, only you were part of it all.'

'How's Margot?'

'She's all right – *Margot Metroland.* D'you mind if I take another drink?'

'I suppose not.'

'Viscountess Metroland,' said Peter. 'What a name! What a man! Still, she's got Alastair all the time. Metroland doesn't mind. He's got what he wanted. I don't see much of them really. What do you do all the time, Paul?'

'I'm going to be ordained soon.'

'Wish I didn't feel so damned ill. What were we saying? Oh yes, about Metroland. You know, Paul, I think it was a mistake you ever got mixed up with us; don't you? We're different somehow. Don't quite know how. Don't think that's rude, do you, Paul?'

'No, I know exactly what you mean. You're dynamic, and I'm static.'

'Is that it? Expect you're right. Funny thing you used to teach me once; d'you remember? Llanabba – Latin sentences, *Quominus* and *Quin*, and the organ; d'you remember?'

'Yes, I remember,' said Paul.

'Funny how things happen. You used to teach me the organ; d'you remember?'

'Yes, I remember,' said Paul.

'And then Margot Metroland wanted to marry you; d'you remember?'

'Yes,' said Paul.

'And then you went to prison, and Alastair – that's Margot Metroland's young man – and Metroland – that's her husband – got you out; d'you remember?'

'Yes,' said Paul, 'I remember.'

'And here we are talking to one another like this, up here, after all that! Funny, isn't it?'

'Yes, it is rather.'

'Paul, do you remember a thing you said once at the Ritz – Alastair was there – that's Margot Metroland's young man, you know – d'you remember? I was rather tight then too. You said, "Fortune, a much-maligned lady." D'you remember that?'

'Yes,' said Paul, 'I remember.'

'Good old Paul! I knew you would. Let's drink to that now; shall we? How did it go? Damn, I've forgotten it. Never mind. I wish I didn't feel so ill.'

'You drink too much, Peter.'

'Oh, damn, what else is there to do? You going to be a clergyman, Paul?'

'Yes.'

'Damned funny that. You know you ought never to have got mixed up with me and Metroland. May I have another drink?'

'Time you went to bed, Peter, don't you think?'

'Yes, I suppose it is. Didn't mind my coming in, did you? After all, you used to teach me the organ; d'you remember? Thanks for the whisky!'

So Peter went out, and Paul settled down again in his chair. So the ascetic Ebionites used to turn towards Jerusalem when they prayed. Paul made a note of it. Quite right to suppress them. Then he turned out the light and went into his bedroom to sleep.

TITLES IN EVERYMAN'S LIBRARY

CHINUA ACHEBE
Things Fall Apart

THE ARABIAN NIGHTS
(tr. Husain Haddawy)

MARCUS AURELIUS
Meditations

JANE AUSTEN
Emma
Mansfield Park
Northanger Abbey
Persuasion
Pride and Prejudice
Sense and Sensibility

HONORÉ DE BALZAC
Cousin Bette
Eugénie Grandet
Old Goriot

SIMONE DE BEAUVOIR
The Second Sex

WILLIAM BLAKE
Poems and Prophecies

JORGE LUIS BORGES
Fictions

JAMES BOSWELL
The Life of Samuel Johnson

CHARLOTTE BRONTË
Jane Eyre
Villette

EMILY BRONTË
Wuthering Heights

MIKHAIL BULGAKOV
The Master and Margarita

SAMUEL BUTLER
The Way of all Flesh

ITALO CALVINO
If on a winter's night a traveler

ALBERT CAMUS
The Stranger

WILLA CATHER
Death Comes for the Archbishop

MIGUEL DE CERVANTES
Don Quixote

GEOFFREY CHAUCER
Canterbury Tales

ANTON CHEKHOV
The Steppe and Other Stories
My Life and Other Stories

KATE CHOPIN
The Awakening

CARL VON CLAUSEWITZ
On War

SAMUEL TAYLOR COLERIDGE
Poems

WILLIAM WILKIE COLLINS
The Moonstone
The Woman in White

JOSEPH CONRAD
Lord Jim
Nostromo
Typhoon and Other Stories
Under Western Eyes
The Secret Agent

DANIEL DEFOE
Moll Flanders
Robinson Crusoe

CHARLES DICKENS
Bleak House
David Copperfield
Great Expectations
Hard Times
Little Dorrit
Oliver Twist
A Tale of Two Cities

DENIS DIDEROT
Memoirs of a Nun

JOHN DONNE
The Complete English Poems

FYODOR DOSTOEVSKY
The Brothers Karamazov
Crime and Punishment

MURASAKI SHIKIBU
The Tale of Genji

VLADIMIR NABOKOV
Lolita
Pale Fire

GEORGE ORWELL
Animal Farm
Nineteen Eighty-Four

BORIS PASTERNAK
Doctor Zhivago

PLATO
The Republic

EDGAR ALLEN POE
The Complete Stories

ALEXANDER PUSHKIN
The Captain's Daughter
and Other Stories

JEAN-JACQUES ROUSSEAU
Confessions

WILLIAM SHAKESPEARE
Sonnets and Narrative Poems
Tragedies Vol. 1

MARY SHELLEY
Frankenstein

ADAM SMITH
The Wealth of Nations

STENDHAL
The Charterhouse of Parma
Scarlet and Black

JOHN STEINBECK
The Grapes of Wrath

LAURENCE STERNE
Tristram Shandy

ROBERT LOUIS STEVENSON
The Master of Ballantrae and Weir of
Hermiston
Dr Jekyll and Mr Hyde
and Other Stories

JONATHAN SWIFT
Gulliver's Travels

JUNICHIRŌ TANIZAKI
The Makioka Sisters

WILLIAM MAKEPEACE
THACKERAY
Vanity Fair

LEO TOLSTOY
Anna Karenina
Childhood, Boyhood and Youth
War and Peace

ANTHONY TROLLOPE
Barchester Towers
The Eustace Diamonds
The Warden

IVAN TURGENEV
Fathers and Children
A Sportsman's Notebook

MARK TWAIN
Tom Sawyer
and Huckleberry Finn

HENRY DAVID THOREAU
Walden

VIRGIL
The Aeneid

VOLTAIRE
Candide

EVELYN WAUGH
Decline and Fall

EDITH WHARTON
The House of Mirth

OSCAR WILDE
Plays, Prose Writings and Poems

MARY WOLLSTONECRAFT
A Vindication of the Rights of
Woman

VIRGINIA WOOLF
To the Lighthouse
Mrs Dalloway

ÉMILE ZOLA
Germinal